tap dancing
derek hartley

teach yourself ®

tap dancing
derek hartley

forewords by wayne sleep
and sylvia young o.b.e.

The author and publisher take no responsibility for accident, injury or any other consequence of following the dances herein. Students practise at their own risk.

For UK order enquiries: please contact Bookpoint Ltd, 130 Milton Park, Abingdon, Oxon OX14 4SB. Telephone: +44 (0) 1235 827720. Fax: +44 (0) 1235 400454. Lines are open 09.00–17.00, Monday to Saturday, with a 24-hour message answering service. Details about our titles and how to order are available at www.teachyourself.co.uk

For USA order enquiries: please contact McGraw-Hill Customer Services, PO Box 545, Blacklick, OH 43004-0545, USA. Telephone: 1-800-722-4726. Fax: 1-614-755-5645.

For Canada order enquiries: please contact McGraw-Hill Ryerson Ltd, 300 Water St, Whitby, Ontario L1N 9B6, Canada. Telephone: 905 430 5000. Fax: 905 430 5020.

Long renowned as the authoritative source for self-guided learning – with more than 50 million copies sold worldwide – the **teach yourself** series includes over 500 titles in the fields of languages, crafts, hobbies, business, computing and education.

British Library Cataloguing in Publication Data: a catalogue record for this title is available from the British Library.

Library of Congress Catalog Card Number: on file.

First published in UK 2007 by Hodder Education, 338 Euston Road, London, NW1 3BH.

First published in US 2007 by the McGraw-Hill Companies, Inc.

This edition published 2007.

The **teach yourself** name is a registered trade mark of Hodder Headline.

Typeset by Pantek Arts Ltd, Maidstone, Kent.
Printed and bound in Spain.

The publisher has used its best endeavours to ensure that the URLs for external websites referred to in this book are correct and active at the time of going to press. However, the publisher and the author have no responsibility for the websites and can make no guarantee that a site will remain live or that the content will remain relevant, decent or appropriate.

Impression number   10 9 8 7 6 5 4 3 2 1

Year   2010 2009 2008 2007

contents

I have trained in most Western disciplines of dance and the one from which I now get the most joy is tap.

I have known Derek Hartley for over 25 years, have been taught and choreographed by him, and we have danced together on stage. He is a born teacher who I cannot recommend too highly. He has invented his own method of teaching, based on the American way, which, for me, is the best.

Many of Derek's approaches are wholly original and he obviously has a great love for his subject. He makes it all sound attainable.

I just know you will enjoy reading this book, be you beginner or experienced tap dancer, and the beauty of learning to tap dance is that you can begin at any age. All the basic sounds and rhythms – thanks to this book – can be achieved very quickly. So get on with it and, as the song says, 'Tap Your Troubles Away!'

Wayne Sleep

Having known Derek for many years I can only say it is with great delight that I write these simple words to introduce you to a fabulous tap dancer and teacher. I know you will enjoy the chance to learn from his methods in this amazing book.

Derek's experience as a teacher could not be greater. He has taught widely at all levels in the profession … youngsters learning their trade; professional dancers; individuals of all ages who enjoy dance and especially tap.

He works his classes hard and demands high standards. He gets to know his students in order to motivate them and he builds self-confidence as well as ability.

Tap dancing is an important part of a performing style, which I love. There is precision, rhythm and expression. It is a high-energy medium and when that energy builds there is a tremendous feeling released, a positive upbeat mood, a zest for life.

It is also a disciplined art form. You have to learn the steps and you have to practise them before you can perform them. There is a lot of hard work behind the successful performance and that's the beauty of it. You make it look as if it's easy.

This book will provide you with the opportunity to learn from Derek's experience. It is fun, it is challenging and if you work at it you will be rewarded. You will feel fitter with the sort of exercise that really gets the muscles moving, but you will also connect with your inner energy.

So, put on your tap shoes, switch on the music and start today!

Sylvia Young O.B.E.

acknowledgements

In my 27 years or so of teaching, performing, choreographing, directing and producing I have come across some very strange characters. I think sometimes a tap class attracts the needy and lost – sorry, not you! I have seen (very) tall men in short shorts, so that my eyes are distracted somewhat; ladies with wild expressions on their faces as they struggle along; nervous shakers, who have the wrong sort of rhythm; people on the wrong side of a drink or two; those who have not given a thought to the point of a tap class and have turned up in flip flops (or hiking boots) and one person who had her toe tap *under the ball of her foot* because she said it was too big for the toe area so she moved it down the shoe until it did fit – on the ball! I'm not making this bit up.

I acknowledge all of these great characters and many, many more who have made me smile just to have them in front of me. I can honestly say I have given all-comers equal time and patience. Even the man who was a little drunk and acted as an echo on every step.

They pale into insignificance, however, beside the people who have attended my classes for years and years, always knowing they will have a good and mentally challenging time and leave with another new experience. Every class is a meeting of minds, a fresh start to the day for some and a way of removing the world from their shoulders, just for an hour.

So thanks to Beverly, Jane, Caroline, Ann, Trish, Wendy, Frances, Sabine, Sally, Liz, Victoria, Jan, Larry, Joy, Sue, Rose, Diane, Emilie, Helen, Maria, Sandra, Dawn, Lisa, Veronique, Sharon, Erico, Andrew, Barry and Nikki. And please forgive me if I have left off your name as a member of my class. There really have been 25,000 classes (so how many people is that, then?).

Very, very special thanks to my incredible dance compadres of the last 25 years (longer than anybody!). My first Tap Company, 'Hartley's Hot Tap' – Diane, Mandy and Richard. What great and wonderful times dancing with them, all over the country and on television.

I want to specifically and honourably thank my friend and co-conspirator Diane Hampstead, without whom I would still be swearing! She is a one-woman steering committee, with an eagle eye and an even sharper pair of feet. Proofreading should be her paid profession because tap dancing she can do already better than anybody. Thank you so much.

I have a friend of long-standing, Joan Nowlan, who is also my stalwart PA that I can call upon at any time. I simply could not have done the amount I have over the last few years without her help. Thank you.

Sue Cygan has been a steadfast friend and light and breezy tapper in my class for over 20 years. She is also great with a computer! Thanks Sue.

Thanks also to …

The fabulous and everlasting Debbie Moore of the Pineapple Dance Centre in Covent Garden, London. This incredible place has been like a second home for over 26 years! I was there at the beginning, in 1979, and maybe I will be there at the end. To all of the other numerous dance centres around the world who have also invited me across the years.

All of the people who have believed in me and my way of doing things. They have all been responsible for this book. It is they who have kept me on my toes long enough to be able to write it.

To Ann Oliver, a friend in the dance world for about 28 years, and her husband 'Edwardo'; the principals of the uncountable number of colleges and the heads of schools who have invited me to teach their children and young dancers; Loraine Grayston for her friendship; my two tap models, Daniel Oates and Adele Taylor for their professionalism and patience. To Sylvia Young and, of course, my good friend Wayne Sleep.

To all of the people who have been to see me and hopefully enjoyed my particular approach to tap. I was inspired as I will go on to say, by my teacher, who was taught by a great choreographer called Buddy Bradley. When I found out it was he who almost single-handedly blended Rhythm tap and European tap (or 'folk tap', shall we say?), I thought that was the way to go myself. What a good idea to blend styles and produce my own! And that is exactly what I have been doing ever since. So, I guess I have to thank tap dance itself!

Hope you like it!

CD track list

The accompanying CD covers the following:

1 Melody 1	20 Paddles sound	39 Double Time Step
2 Warm-up 1	21 Paddle Step sound	40 Triple Time Step
3 Warm-up 2	22 Paddle Step Heel sound	41 Quadruple Time Step
4 Warm-up 3	23 3 Beat Paddle sound	42 Single Time Step Break
5 Shuffles 123	24 Paddle Step In Triplet sound	43 Double Time Step Break
6 Ball Heel 123	25 4 Beat Paddle sound	44 Triple Time Step Break
7 Shuffle Step 123	26 5 Beat Paddle sound	45 Quadruple Time Step Break
8 Shuffle Step Heel 123	27 6 Beat Paddle sound	46 Triple Time Step and Break sound
9 Counting explained	28 7 Beat Paddle sound	47 Shim Sham 1 sound
10 Syncopation explained	29 8 Beat Paddle sound	48 Shim Sham 2 sound
11 Melody 2	30 3 Beat Riff sound	49 Shim Sham 3 sound
12 Melody 3	31 4 Beat Riff sound	50 Shim Sham 4 sound
13 Melody 4	32 5 Beat Riff sound	51 Hartley Shim Sham 4 sound
14 Melody 5	33 6 Beat Riff sound	52 Combination 1
15 Melody 6	34 7 Beat Riff sound	53 Combination 2
16 Melody 7	35 Buffalo sound	54 Combination 3
17 Shuffles sound	36 Maxie Ford sound	55 Amalgamation 1
18 Shuffle Step sound	37 Maxie Ford with pick-up sound	56 Amalgamation 2
19 Shuffle Step Heel sound	38 Single Time Step	57 Amalgamation 3

What to buy as music to tap dance to

Jazz music for the timing in 4/4. This is deliberately a general term because the choices are so vast. Begin with the names of musicians you recognize and admire. Try the current and 'new' jazz names. These may be younger artists with a strong link to this type of music, despite their age. They are refreshing and can give new feeling to traditional and well-known pieces as well as inspire with some great original work.

Listen to famous singers such as Sinatra or Ella Fitzgerald, Stevie Wonder, Billy Joel, David Bowie and Harry Connick Jr. Don't forget the classics such as Fred Astaire, Fats Waller and Louis Armstrong because it was in this era that music was written to dance to! You can't help but dance when you have this kind of swing playing.

introduction

For many years I toyed with the idea of producing a video about teaching tap dance, but I always resisted because I thought, where is a video machine usually kept? In the living room at home, or at least in a place where there would probably be a carpet. So, what would be the point of a video without a wooden floor in front of the player on which to imitate what you would be watching? Nevertheless, I always wanted to do it. Perhaps somebody should have convinced me.

But a book, and here I am most grateful to have been asked by Hodder Education, now that is interesting! It is a challenge just to get a dance medium across that is almost entirely sound based via the written page. I have never really felt it was an easy thing to do, especially as it would have to involve reading all of the foot instructions and the counts – wow! And there have been books before, not to mention all of the usual dance syllabi; what could I bring that would be different? But then I remembered, I have always wanted to give my particular ideas, gained over so many years, a wider airing. So, here I am and I hope I have done a good job. I have written it to entertain as well as inform. Let's say this is Teach Yourself Tap Dance My Way!

Looking at other books was not something I did until after I had completed at least half of this book. They can be confusing and hard to fathom but having read a couple, I was given more confidence to press on with mine. I have light-heartedly directed you through a book of facts as well as figures and led you to believe that you can tap dance too. I decided to simply put down all of those ideas, asides, anecdotes, opinions and facts that have occurred or happened to me over the past 25 years at the top of my game, either from meeting people or just from expanding my own mind.

I have always wanted to do it all my way. Tap dancing *with a style* is what I have always pursued, not because I disagreed with other ways but because it just kept on bursting out of me. I think that my way – for me – is the more honest way and the only way I could have done it. I have been dancing, singing, choreographing, teaching, directing and producing shows, and especially tap dance shows, since about 1980. Before that I was a professional dancer and before that I was a ballroom and Latin dancer, gaining considerable success when I was in my teens.

I made my mother, and especially my father, very proud when I was winning all those competitions with my beautiful partner!

Being a male professional dancer from a northern English city and with working class credentials firmly in place, it could be assumed that I probably kept the fact under wraps, especially at school. But I had no problem with it at all. Can I state here and now that I simply regarded dancing as another form of activity; almost a sport. In fact, I was a good decathlete at club level at the same time as I was going to dance classes.

It was something I found so easy to pick up. I don't know why; it was just so. What I do know is that I was always watching Fred Astaire and Gene Kelly on television and I couldn't wait to try out the moves I was seeing. It was simply very exciting to watch two men being so fit and clever, not to mention the glow that goes with knowing that as a good male dancer you are always in demand to dance with the ladies in your life! I have been dancing thus for the past 40 years in total.

The tap dancing came about because I also discovered I had natural energy and rhythm. My mother's favourite expression was 'go outside and do something!', which meant I was free to go anywhere. I was to be found running and jumping all over the local woods and fields, building up my great stores of energy.

Unbeknown to me at the time, my grandfather's sister was on the stage in the old Music Hall days around Manchester; that, as far as I could see, was the only connection I had with dancing and singing. My mother was always singing around the house, and of course in her young days between the wars and after, almost every household had a piano in the sitting room and I know her brothers and sisters were always around that piano – and the ones in the pubs probably.

There was no television, and no CD player and video and little radio even. But there were some amazing acts around in those times and I have spent many happy days reading about great people from the past who had such hard but interesting lives. The books I have read about the acts in early American vaudeville days give such incredible facts about life on the road and what they went through to survive. I now give lectures on these historical facts to future dancers in their colleges! See the taking it further chapter at the end of this book.

As a child I didn't know any of this but whenever something like it came on to our first ever television I would be watching it, entranced. When I finally got into dancing proper, and became the professional I always wanted to be, I was taken over by the possibilities open to me. What a way to go through a life, I thought, enjoying yourself all the time! Dancing for a living! Could there *be* a better way?

Around the age of 17, I decided to try to dance for a living, somehow, some way. I started the ballroom and the Latin and soon discovered I was able to pick it all up with ease. I am still dancing some 40 years later. I am still performing, still teaching and lecturing, still enjoying the gift I was given. It has been a fantastic journey even thus far and I am so grateful to have done it all. There is still much to do.

At the same time, dance can be a harsh mistress; ask any dancer. Dancing as a living is difficult and somewhat perverse. Well, who wants to willingly go through a punishing exercise routine of stretching and pulling and pushing the body to do often impossible things – and for hours every day – then go back into a class the next day with all of the groans and pains and do it all again? That has to be some kind of weird, right?

Ask any professional dancer if they enjoy the pain and they will say yes, they do. I speak, I believe, for all working dancers, young or old and male or female and from anywhere in the world when I say that to be in touch with all of your physicality at all times is truly a gift from God. And you *must* be in touch, to do dance as a profession.

I also believe that *anyone* who really enjoys going to their dancing classes can feel this too.

If you were to decide on a purpose to fully use yourself up in life and to let no day go by without fulfilling your time on earth, as I did as a child, you could do worse than be a dancer. How else can you completely utilize everything you have, both physically and mentally? All is used in dance and all is needed. You are *fully* engaged and you can indeed 'fly' at times, such is the excitement it can give you. It can become all you want to do, and that actually happened to me. I thought that to be as fit and as fast and as light and as strong as possible would be such a great thing!

My father spent his entire life unwell and at times extremely ill. But his spirit was what I inherited and I have to thank him so much here. Family life was tough in those days and I therefore dedicate this book to my parents.

I remember when my first contract arrived in the post, after an impromptu and unofficial audition for Butlin's Holidays. It was amazing to have this Equity contract in my hand and it meant I would become a professional and come out of the amateur ballroom world. I was 19 years old, and I asked my father what he thought of his son becoming a real dancer. He simply said, 'Whatever you want to do, son, is okay by us. We'll support you all the way.'

Thanks Dad. Love, Derek.

01 who? what? why? where? how?

In this chapter you will learn:

- about shoes and equipment
- about where to learn
- how to get started.

If I say this chapter is about a lot of loose change, but is still very important currency just the same, that will serve as a good introduction to it. It is to entice you further into a world of great enjoyment and no small amount of excitement. I can say this because today and for many years, I still hear from my class cries of, 'Yes!' or 'I got it!' – or I just see a huge collective smile when they are looking in the mirror in the studio and actually tap dancing!

When a tap class is in full flow and everyone is doing the same thing and with the same rhythm, it is joyful to be in it. It is joyful to hear it, too. The number of times people stop and look as they pass the studio door because the sound has stopped them in their tracks (especially if an unusual piece of music is being played) is huge. It manages to achieve a sort of magical hold on participator and spectator. It can look easy to the untrained eye (or feet) but the ones doing the steps know they are learning something very special.

Who is this book for?

Who are these people who come to a tap class? Who are *you*, dear reader, who has bought this book? Who are you out to please with this task? Of course, you are out to please **yourself**.

You are anyone and everyone because that is who can learn to tap dance. You are young, old, male or female and you have chosen this book because you have either tap danced previously and want to get back into it; or you 'have always wanted to do it'.

I have encountered many reasons people have for wanting to tap dance, in my career: 'I need it because it's my therapy'; 'I used to be good at this'; 'My mother never let me go to a dance class'; 'It will keep me fit'; 'It will get me out of the house'; 'It's something *for me*'. The common thing is, each person wants to please their *self*; wants to please their ears and eyes and their heart and their soul. No! It isn't far-fetched or unreal, it's actually true.

In a class, there are professional people such as doctors, anaesthetists, publishers, bank managers, secretaries, nurses, airline personnel, heads of companies, students (of all kinds), housewives, husbands, singers, actors, musicians, dancers and children. I sometimes wonder why they are all so different and yet so alike.

I ask them outright, 'Why are you doing this?', especially when I watch their faces and see such a struggle going on sometimes! They can look so worried in their concentration and enjoyment but it's just their way of rising to the challenge. They don't really have to answer my question because it's there in the search for perfection. I am the one who is often lost for words – in admiration.

Well, that is *you*. Who am I?

That's easy. I am the one who can help you to realize your dream of being able to tap dance. Ready? Okay, then ... read on!

What to wear?

In a tap class or at home practising as an adult tapper, the thing to wear is – why don't I tell you first what *not* to wear? A *leotard and tights*! Got that, lads?

These belong to the old perception of tap dancing, long ago passed as far as I am concerned, though I dare say some teachers out there still encourage this outrageous dress. Nothing, for me, would say more about the worst aspects of tap dancing than this wrong dress code, and that code includes shoes too. Maybe tap was danced like that once upon a time, but not since the 1930s. Today tap is a modern dance, done to modern music as well as to classic tracks, and so it looks best in simple clothing of today. It's the twenty-first century, right?

For the men, slacks or tracksuit bottoms and a t-shirt or shirt. For the women, if not the same, then dance trousers, and usually in black. Really, however, the more colourful the top or dress code, the better the disposition to learn. I always think one plays better tennis when wearing white, don't you?

So, loose clothing is ideal. Dare I suggest a skirt or dress for women? If you were learning ballroom or Latin, it would be a dress or similar and nobody would think anything of it. Ginger Rogers and Rita Hayworth and other iconic movie stars didn't look too bad in them! It is obviously down to what you prefer, but nothing too tight.

Mentioning old movie stars might give the impression that tap is still fixed in the past. Well, it is – and it isn't – but that is the point of it. I mean how old is music?

Now for the shoes!

This is a serious area because tap shoes can last a long time! If you buy the wrong ones you will have them for years, because only a professional tapper will wear out a pair of tap shoes. Some people come to class with tap shoes that their grandmother used to wear! They really can last, those shoes!

It is possible to simply use a comfortable pair of your own ordinary shoes and buy the taps to put on them. You can, of course, begin the lessons today with just such a pair of shoes *but* I must say that I have rarely seen this work, not least because the slightest wear on the heel or sole will mean that it isn't flat enough leather – and it has to be leather – for the metal taps to sit on them snugly. One thing you should certainly *not* buy is shoes with the taps riveted on! They must be screw-fixed.

Therefore, put in some practice with this book before you spend a huge amount of money on tap shoes. You can achieve lots of good sounds with leather-soled, standard or 'Oxford' type shoes. It is fashionable today to wear the sort of unisex tap shoes in class and not high heels or strap-fastening shoes. You would wear such shoes if you were learning to ballroom dance and of course you can tap in them if they are preferred.

It also depends on your own comfort, but if a high heel is worn your ankle is already set in a pointed position and so flexibility is hindered.

A better pair of shoes is one with a medium-sized heel and a rounded toe, and again in leather. Some soles are made from a composite material and are too soft to hold on to the screws that fix the taps. Even some purpose-made tap shoes have this awful material as the sole and should be avoided. Tap shoe soles must be leather only, and I mean sole *and* heel. No plastic heels if possible!

The taps themselves are also important and can be bought separately. I have always used the American Capezio Tele Tone Taps because they have a particularly clever sound. The screws, three to toe and three to heel, fix the tap to the shoe but go through a soundboard, specially designed to react with the taps. This piece of material is the same shape as the toe and heel taps and provides the hard surface for them to beat against. Cleverly, the screws are meant to be loosened enough to gain the sort of sound you desire.

By doing this, a tiny gap is created between the tap and the soundboard and – similarly to castanets – the sound is rounded within two convex surfaces (Tele Tones have convex surfaces). The difference, if the screws are tightened right down, is really obvious. Loosening is like 'tuning' the taps and I have seen many a relieved look on the face of a dancer when this loosening is done on their shoes. They are suddenly able to hear their efforts!

Other makes of tap shoe, such as Bloch and the American shoes, Leo's 'Alexander Concerto' (you will probably have to order these), come with taps already attached. These are very good shoes and I can recommend them. Some Capezio tap shoes come with just one central tuning screw! A clever idea and it may impress you enough to buy them.

I have had shoes hand-made and they are always going to be the best. Another American shoe by Capezio is called a 'K360' and they are *the* most expensive at time of writing, at about $200 – and in the UK, actually £250. They come in the same design for all sizes and can have built-up toes to give a really loud and clean sound. Tap shoes like these are the result of much research and development and can be the dancer's dream when they are found. I have spent years searching for the wonderful shoe that will make me better. I go on!

Many shoes, like the K360, are now built up at the toe and actually look like they have three or four soles – and that is because they do. This gives weight to the front of the shoe and I am always telling my classes to imagine they have 'heavy toes' and to bounce them off the floor. I now wear this type and after getting used to them have almost accepted my great search is over!

The dancewear shops that stock a few makes are the ones to check out, to see what works for you. These may be with or without taps, cheap or expensive. I know of a cheap canvas shoe that some people would not change at all. Do not buy those shoes with a pointed toe and an inward sloping high-ish heel that is also set in a 'turned-up toe' position. Rather, shoes should be flexible and with a larger heel and rounded toe shape for the tap. If you like the shoes on sale but they are without taps you will need to pay extra for the taps and then have them fitted. Do not get permanently fixed taps because you cannot tune them.

Another shoe I cannot really get on with is the trainer shoe or jazz trainer type tap shoe. It looks modern but always sounds very dull because the tap is hitting against a rubber (!) sole. In my opinion, this entirely defeats the principle I have just described where a leather sole is essential. An even worse example is the tap trainer boot! This will certainly hold the ankle very still – which is just what a tap dancer needs – not! Two bad points there, in one shoe, for me.

Another jazz type dance shoe is the split sole variety with no support at all between sole and heel underneath. The only thing that joins top to sole is stitching. They look really good but I couldn't recommend them to anyone but an advanced dancer, because only they would do them justice.

The New Yorker is a performance shoe with a high heel and a pointed toe! Also, it fastens with a strap. However, it is a traditional stage shoe and can look very professional. For a beginner, though, I would doubt they would serve. In the end, they are your feet and you may not be able to wear high (or low) heels under any circumstances. Try a few to suit and get what you need.

The best way to illustrate this is with a story of a man who came into a beginners' class with a pair of sparkly red very high heels! I did ask why and he gave a very good answer. He was going to star in a pantomime as a Dame and wanted to get into the shoes as quickly as possible. What a perfect shoe for him!

Looking at a person's tap shoes in a class tells me a lot about them as a tap dancer. Whether or not they are right for that person, or whether they are getting in the way. Or is the person actually too good for the poor shoes they have on their feet; that is so common. You must avoid buying a pair of anything until you become more certain about where your weight is. Is it forward or back? Are you heavy or light? Are you heavy or light but the opposite when dancing (a light person with a heavy way of landing)? Try to judge for yourself and buy light shoes if you're heavy and heavy shoes if you are smaller and lighter.

When you finally decide, do 'tune' your taps. By loosening just the front screw of the three it is possible to tap them with your fingers and hear a sort of hollowness, but they should not rattle when you shake them. Do the rattle and finger test when next dancing in your studio! Same for both toe and heel taps.

Now, just a few words about other equipment you will need to begin your dance journey.

You may need a chair for your balance, especially when concentrating intently. This is fine, but if you do not have a chair (I mean you will have a chair, but it may not be in the place you're practising) hold on to something, even the wall. Although to be frank, your balance will improve with practice.

For music, you will need a player; even the radio is a great source of ad hoc rhythms you can use endlessly. I must also add that dancing to your own music that you have at home will give you a new perspective on that music. It will give you an added dimension to learning to tap dance.

A good aid is a tape recorder or a dictaphone. You can replay yourself or if going to a class, record the class. You must ask, of course! The same for a video camera – and you absolutely must ask in this case. Only ever film a teacher's class with express permission. Private lessons are the places to do this.

Finally, the mirror. Not to be used for looking at, but for looking *into*. You are correcting or helping the figure in the mirror and using it for line and style; you are not looking at yourself. Also, the mirror confirms you are doing the steps! You therefore have a double confirmation – hearing yourself and seeing yourself too!

Even at feet level, the mirror should be useful, to get ankles and angles as right as possible and to see your imaginary centre line to generally equalize yourself.

Try to think like a juggler, who looks straight ahead while also looking at the balls in the air; not looking at each hand in turn, but looking at each hand *at the same time*. Try to equalize yourself in the feet in the same sort of way. Feel like you are getting in touch with a kind of inner self because it is going to be *you* who is listening to you doing this.

Why tap dance?

I guess it will depend on what kind of person you are to begin with to answer that question 'Why am I doing this?' As I said earlier, it literally takes all sorts. I think that all of these sorts have one thing in common, however; the search for the kind of skill that is based in music but that does not call for an instrument. Only the feet are required, at first. So, no piano, no guitar, no set of drums, no saxophone to drag around for lessons. Just your shoes.

I asked one of my students at the Pineapple Dance Centre in London to give me her reasons for learning to tap in a class. This is what she told me in a letter:

It takes focus, so you forget your troubles. It keeps the brain active and the interest alive, which I miss in running and swimming for instance. I could truly tap for hours because the fun factor is much higher than the intention of just merely keeping fit. Tap also possesses a glorious paradox of solitude and togetherness. I become aware of a strong group connection as we learn the routine singularly, yet we dance it very much together.

We seem to dance to everything and I find this stays with me long after the lesson has finished. There is always something to take away from each class to practise at home and this leads to a real sense of achievement and skill development. I've only been tapping for about four months and have seen myself progress over that time. Tap has so easily slotted into my lifestyle and is something I wouldn't want to lose now.

Debbie Y. (2006)

Thanks Debbie, I am most grateful to you for putting it into your own words.

We all have rhythm; the rhythm of life itself. Maybe those of us who tap dance actually have a kind of deep love for ourselves. You have to like yourself to be able to express yourself, I think. Some of us sing, some of us paint, or write, or build or compose or act. Some of us tailor or sculpt or cook. All of these are great artistic endeavours and forms of expressing our own self; getting out what is inside. If it's rhythm you've got, get it out – somehow, some way.

I like dancers and people who just dance. In particular I feel proud when men turn up to a tap class full of women – and stay to learn. That happened to me in a Cordon Bleu cookery course in evening classes. The only man there – expected to fail, stayed the whole year! If you've just got to get the rhythm out, what better way than to stick on a pair of tap shoes and tap yourself happy. In fact, you cannot stay in a bad mood once you start to tap dance! It's not possible to tap unhappy.

Therefore, I do think you – secretly even – like yourself! I think you're artistic and I think you're in search of expression. I think that is why I welcome you to the club.

Do it for all of the reasons I have mentioned, but most of all … do it for yourself.

Where?

I hope you agree that one of the results of using this book will prove to be a good start to learning this dance skill. Tap has such a chequered history and has touched so many lives throughout time, not least those who just enjoy watching it. It really can stir something within you; to go on and do it yourself is a bonus you will love.

Then where do you practise? First of all, you have to practise *in your feet* and *in your head*. Find a floor in your home or, if you have your own dance studio or small ballroom, try to justify having such a space and use it to practise! Don't keep it just for special occasions. No! Use it! Either that or – the kitchen floor.

It's usually the hardest floor in the house and will give back a decent sound. Even a flat has a kitchen floor but if you do live over someone, *no* tap shoes! Even slippers will do!

Of course, a class, whether public or private lessons, should be your next consideration and seeking them out locally is maybe your best path after this book.

Even when you have begun lessons, however, it is essential to practise in your own time. You can easily and cheaply buy a board to practise on. You would have your very own 'floor drum' and it can be put away afterwards. It only needs to be a metre square and about 15 mm thick to make sure it does not bend or warp. You can endlessly beat up this piece of wood and really enjoy a cathartic stress-busting hour or so!

In all of this your success will depend a great deal on having the right teacher, and by that I mean the right teacher for you.

Who knows who gets on with whom? In my own case, I can feel certain I have just given a good class, and good enough to get people to return next week; but it isn't always so. The class could just as easily have seemed too hard for some. Those people don't come back a week later, or at all. There is no way of telling, until you try, who will do it for you.

If you do not have a dance centre in your city – and there are quite a few nowadays – find a local dance school, because they may have adult tap classes in the evening. As I explain throughout, I don't teach a 'syllabus' style, and this book will not necessarily recommend one. However, I wouldn't be fair to you, the reader, if I didn't give you every chance. I think more about tap dancing than to be too prejudiced.

So, first seek out a teacher and check what style she or he is doing.

Some will teach tap with titles, such as Adult Bronze, Silver or Gold medals, etc. I know nothing about these personally but can only speak about some results I have seen. I guess I just don't like to see very large children tap dancing, i.e. adults doing childish steps, with accompanying unnecessary arms to boot. I give the adult learner more credit, I hope, and don't want them to look foolish. Whatever class you choose, check out the teacher and go for their open or freestyle class, if you can, and if they are doing one!

Get to know the real deal. Tap should be sassy and cute, low down and groovy, cool and classy, not a remake of your child's grades. If the teacher treats you like an adult, they're the one. Simple.

You know, I thought I could already tap dance when I looked for a teacher in the *Stage* newspaper one day, years ago. I wanted to find a teacher giving private lessons. I found one and went along – and in five minutes with a lady called Joy Adams, I realized I couldn't tap. I was shocked but absolutely elated. I had found my teacher and there was only her from that moment. This was in 1977 and Joy was in her sixties then, I think. God bless her soles if she has now passed on, for I do not know her whereabouts. If she is still alive all these years later I hope she is well – and still dancing!

You see, before her I only knew a syllabus style myself. She, however, was a direct connection to the real thing because she was a student of the late Buddy Bradley. My future began then because I could see this was *the real deal*. Read more about the great Buddy Bradley later.

How?

How fit should you be? How fit will you become? How long will it take to learn? How often should you practise? There are many answers.

Regarding your fitness, you could be as fit or as unfit and overweight as you like. In tap dance it sort of doesn't matter, which is why a lot of people like to learn it. Obviously check out your back, lower back, knees, hips and feet, and get advice if you are not sure about dancing. Tap is pretty static at this stage, so I don't regard fitness or lack of it as a worry.

My oldest student, as I write, is 90 years old. He has private lessons, so no chance for me to relax there then! Rhythm knows no size or height or weight or age. Perish the thought.

How fit will it make you? Well, there you *can* improve. Just practise – and practise. The enjoyment alone will shed pounds and build a better bottom (!) and slim your ankles, and yes, the hips too. You will become stronger and fitter but what people forget is, you also become fit in the head! It's a brain game to tap dance and that's because it is an instrument. Seriously, tap will give you an overall fitness and strengthen your legs and back. If I were to compare it to a specific sport, for instance, it would be to boxing, for its springiness and fast weight transference.

Which brings me neatly to how long will it take you? Can I ask how long does it take to learn to play the piano? Or to play that guitar you may have bought? When you are at an advanced stage with these two instruments, it just begins to really get interesting, right? Of course, 'how long' is not a question here. Therefore there is no answer. It's a lifelong pleasure; you stop tap dancing when you die!

Obviously, we are all different, but I always say that three months of once-a-week classes and your own personal practice should see you mastering all of the basics in this book alone. Also, given peoples' time/work constraints I should still expect good results inside six months. A skill worth learning is a skill worth having. There is no doubt that tap dancing is a skill. As for worth learning, just you try to stop once you start!

I think you have read enough now, to begin, don't you? Off you go then!

02 how do you teach yourself to tap dance?

In this chapter you will learn:

- that you have the main tools for tap
- the four 'R's of tap instruction
- the power of practise.

02

Well, let's think about what we *need* and about what we already *have* in order to tap dance.

Need: ears, eyes, feet, balance, music, space, time, will, hope.

Have: ears, eyes, feet, balance, music, space – you know the rest!

Tap should be as easy as walking on the spot. If you can do that, and keep in time with a given tempo, you should be able to at least begin to Teach Yourself to Tap Dance.

As with all artistic endeavours – and dancing is an artistic endeavour, however you look at it or do it – the basis for success is *observation*. We observe with, of course, the five senses. We need two of these at least here – the eyes and the ears – as well as the sense of touch, for the feet. Most of us have these and if learning to tap dance you will definitely need them.

In all of the time I have been teaching I have realized that everyone 'knows how it should be, it's just doing it that is the problem'. Just like an instrument. You should think of learning to tap dance in the same way as learning to play an instrument. Yes, it is problematic at first but it is the reward that counts. A skill not worked for, remember?

Instructions have to be heard (or seen), then assimilated (the crucial point here); then when the brain is ready it moves the relevant body parts. We all 'know' this, it's just doing it, right?

- **Relax**. It's the same for everybody. And when I use the expression 'this is your left foot, this is your right foot', I really mean that you have to keep on reminding yourself which is which. Believe me, you will not recognize your 'other foot' at first. We all know the other hand 'knows' what to write, but could we get it to do it?

- **Remind**. Tell yourself that only *you* can teach yourself to dance. A set of instructions, a sympathetic voice, an encouragement – all this is necessary. But, it is *your* left foot, it is *your* right foot. You are responsible for them. You must connect. You are learning to control your actions intricately. Up until now, you may have only used your feet for walking and standing.

- **Rewind**. Go over it again and make sure you are not doing it wrong. We can become very good at being wrong, can't we? Try not to practise the wrong way; be sure of the instruction and *listen* and *compare* your feet sounds with those on the CD or in the specifics of the counts and instructions given.

- **Repeat**. Practise. Become obsessed with the desire to be precise. Don't give up, don't ever give up. Amuse yourself with sounding right and looking right. Study the positions on the pages; be pleased with the results.

'**A good singer is always singing.**' Personally, I am always tap dancing. The kitchen, the platform, the shop, the queue, the table (!). It doesn't matter to me. Anywhere counts.

'**See the rhythm, hear the action**' in your head, in your mind.

Train the muscles to memorize. Use the concept of a muscle memory. You are learning a skill after all.

So, what I am trying to do first is to help you to reassure yourself. Practise, as you would any instrument. Be determined to succeed and give yourself little goals to strike off along the way. Gather the information and put it into action anywhere you can to get the muscle memory exercised. But *not* necessarily in your tap shoes! It can be annoying for the neighbours and embarrassing in the supermarket! Ordinary leather-soled shoes will suffice when you are 'always singing'.

03 historical and social aspects

In this chapter you will learn:

- the background
- the style
- the method.

03

For as long as the human has heard his own footsteps, his own voice and the sound of the basic music of the beat from the drum, he has wanted to dance. Evidence on cave walls has proved that primitive man definitely danced, and thus would have created sounds – of his own feet stamping, his own hands clapping; later he would dance to the sound of his own labour.

That labour gradually became more industrialized and as he made his millions of machines he realized that there was a rhythm created by them and within them. He found he could dance to those basic mechanical sounds – and to those of the horseless carriage, and of the streetcar, the looms in the factory and to the sounds of his footfall on the cobbles beneath his feet as he walked to work in his clogs.

Working men and women needed to dance to escape the lives created by the machine-driven culture of their own making. *Dancing is in every one of us* and rhythm is basic to our being alive at all. All cultures dance and have danced and all peoples are in touch with this very primitive strand within.

Tap dancing, however, is distinctly American, though the strands that make it up come from all over the world. Europe and Africa are the two main areas of origin and in Europe we need to specifically look to England and Ireland for the beginnings of tap dance.

The early Irish peasants wore hard shoes, footwear designed for protection against the inclement weather. Maybe to keep warm, maybe to amuse themselves, maybe for no reason at all the inhabitants of Ireland developed their jig, a distinctive step dance with intricate leg movement and footwork. Tapping was done with the toes and heels … with skilful dancers executing as many as fifteen taps in one second.

Across the sea in England, footwork was taking a turn of its own so that by the mid-1770s step dancing began to take on the competitive improvization synonymous with the dance itself. In the manufacturing city of Lancashire, during recreation periods the men and women would dance on the stone streets outside of the mills … and contests were held to see who could produce the most varied sounds and rhythms. As with the Irish jig and reels British clog dancing was distinctive shoe music and upper body movement was eliminated as dancers beat many of the steps that were soon to emigrate to the American stage.

Jerry Ames, *The Book of Tap*, 1977

America has seen centuries of European influx and from the days of the War of Independence the country has accepted people from the four corners of the world. Before this, in slavery's dark days, the Africans' enforced emigration was responsible for the roots of jazz rhythm taking hold in the country of their ominous foreboding. This collision of cultures would prove to be fundamental to the birth of a great nation, even though the reasons were often born of shame, poverty and war.

The Europeans' trek to America, the Africans' infamous journey to America and the West Indies, and the cotton mill workers and the wheels of industry in England all somehow collaborated to put men and women in touch with their inner beat. A heart beat – a rhythm of life!

We tap dance today for the same reasons we did then – escape, entertainment, connection, joy, fitness and communication (for it is a voice, an instrument of the body itself) and whether in a class or by ourselves we can do this thing called tap dance.

I have known famous jazz dancers and choreographers who have said without hesitation, 'If you can't tap dance, as far as I am concerned you can't dance'.

And even the great Fred Astaire remarked, 'I don't know where it comes from ... and I don't want to know!' As if by knowing from whence this well spring occurred he would lose the ability to do it.

Maybe we don't know *why* we dance, or what moves our feet. But we all do it, even unconsciously. To be rhythmic is to be human and tap dance merely expresses our human-ness through this joyful sound. And *everyone* has rhythm – it's just that some people have to search a little harder to find it!

I have proved this time and time again, from teaching people of every age – from six to 90 years; from amateurs to West End stars, such as Peter Bowles and Twiggy; from non-dancers to outright sceptics. And do you know, tap dance is an ultimate leveller – you wouldn't know in a class of tappers just who is the king and who is the pauper. Or, for that matter, where on earth they are from in the world! It's everyone's dance; a dance of the people from so many countries, proved by the amazingly international attendance at some of my classes at the Pineapple Dance Centre in London's Covent Garden.

It's absolutely appropriate that a dance having its roots in folk dance should be a dance of all the folk.

For those who have grown up with the musical films of Hollywood, or with the theatre, or with the children who go to dance classes up and down the country all week and in all weather, tap dancing is very enjoyable – even just to watch. It's infectious, it's engaging, it's wonderful for the spirit and help for the heart.

At the time of writing I am celebrating something of a milestone – 25,000 classes taught to date! Or should that be the 'first 25,000 classes'? Not just in tap of course, but mostly. I say this to illustrate, perhaps, just how long you can expect to be doing this! It's a lifetime's mission of enjoyment, but learnt in a few months.

Every journey, and thus every dance, has a first step. So begin today with step one – just single sounds on your feet.

Read this book, enjoy the journey, make a noise, get in touch ... with yourself. Then let go of yourself ...

come, get together, let the dance floor feel your leather, step as lightly as a feather, let yourself go.

Irving Berlin. Sung by Fred Astaire

About this style

I think it is important to give a brief overview of styles and techniques, so I would like to go into some facts and relevant issues.

Tap has always been laid claim to by two or three sources. African Americans say it is a black dance; the Irish have fiercely defended its origins as theirs and the English have maintained an interest because of clog dancing. Clog has a history all to itself, as does Irish dance and African dance. But tap dance is *all* and *none* of these.

There are those American voices who have always said, and continue to say, that it was stolen from them by the white dancers back in the early days of Minstrelsy. That would be the early nineteenth century, and there is some truth in this claim. However, everybody stole dance moves from everybody else and there were certainly a lot of Irish in the emerging cities of America! The city environment was actually responsible for some of tap's history but the countryside was also responsible – and that was where the poor black settlers were mainly employed before the American Civil War.

You have only to watch early film to see the crossover in the dancers themselves. Those coming to America (the New World) at that time all brought with them their cultural identities. And with these identities came their dances. It is obvious to my eyes that even the great and wonderful Bill 'Bojangles' Robinson himself had a significant Irish influence in his dancing, in feet as well as in body, although he is credited as being one of the black forerunners in the integration of white and black dancing in entertainment all over America.

Therefore, what eventually came about was that a 'New World dance' was born, but from the Old (other) World dances of those millions of people arriving.

> Tap is our American folk dance. It is the red, white and blue. I don't know how else to explain it.
> Eleanor Powell (Foreword) in Jerry Ames,
> *The Book of Tap*, 1977

So much intensity, formed from so diverse a cultural mix, was bound to produce a new and extremely vibrant dance form. This early dance form became known as jazz. Tap was thus the first jazz dance.

Jazz *music* was part of the African soul, with those syncopated and infectious rhythms, but it was formalized and written down by the more savvy and educated Europeans at the time. Later, the descendants of the slave ships from Africa produced their own jazz works, and great musicians such as Eubie Blake, Scott Joplin, Louis Armstrong, Duke Ellington and Fats Waller were merely the more famous of a groundswell of African inspired music and rhythm.

Tap dance was the precursor to jazz music – not the other way around – and was the first performance jazz dance that became popular among street entertainers and travelling tent performers. Before this there was strutting, cakewalking and eccentric dancing to be found everywhere and on every stage. The first really overwhelmingly popular social jazz dance was the Charleston, in the 1920s, a dance every bit as equal in terms of mass following as the Twist in the later 1960s.

Styles are thus created from more than one source and are then subject to embellishment and change. Tap dance has many styles because it is drawn from many sources and although the basic techniques are very similar, what happens after these are learnt is what makes the difference.

So, a shuffle is a shuffle, a heel is a heel. It's the way they are used that denotes the style. It's also very much in the interpretation of the weight distribution. To be brief, styles are, in varying degrees, *in the floor* or *up in the air*. These two states are perfectly encompassed in the flatter floor-bound black American style and the elevated off the floor style of the white Europeans. This European style is essentially Irish but was later further elaborated by the addition of arms and body lines not previously associated with it. Irish dance has no use of arms in tradition.

The former style is more sound based, highly reliant on rhythm and in fact is called 'Rhythm Tap'; its inventor was the fantastic and incomparable black dancer John Bubbles. The latter style is more visually based and is what could loosely be called 'Show Tap'. This is the style of tap dance that is seen on the silver screen of the Hollywood musicals and on the West End stage and Broadway.

Rhythm Tap has a fantastic history and exists despite efforts to marginalize it by the European stylists, and by those in history who would write the formalized versions we see today in a syllabus. They have in many ways impeded tap's original virtuosity, its spontaneity and its soul. There is no Rhythm Tap syllabus for instance, and only lip service is paid by the formal versions currently being practised. They are, I think, ballet-based in their classic approach to learning. Tap dance, being of Jazz origin, loses its feeling if taught this way. The right teacher will, of course, know this and will use their jazz influence to teach the dance.

Perhaps a parallel can be drawn between tango dances. The tango of ballroom origin is very different to that real-life dance, the Argentine tango. One has been formalized, structured and embellished to a great and even ridiculous extent, while the other remains faithful to its roots and has a deeper social connection.

One is definitely a recreation, one is a living thing. Tap has undergone this parallel treatment since the 1930s too.

The tap dance style I use is again a blend of sources and here I must pay homage to my teacher's teacher.

He was a famous black American tap dancer called Buddy Bradley, who came to London in the 1940s and stayed to become the city's foremost tap teacher and choreographer into the 1950s and 1960s. He was a very highly regarded dancer and choreographer and 'rescued' shows in London's West End theatre for such great producers as Noel Coward.

In *The Book of Tap* (McKay 1977), Jerry Ames says that Bradley 'taught the techniques of black hoofers to the emerging group of young white musical performers'. He states that he 'preferred the more exact and drummer-like precision of the white jazz musicians' and that this made it easy to follow and to transform into tap routines. This man can perhaps even be credited with bringing real tap dancing across the Atlantic, because in him was the first mixing of black and white influence to produce the kind of hybrid that everyone fell in love with. A clever and respected man, Buddy Bradley saw the opportunity to unite the basic forms of the dance and was solely responsible for its new direction in the UK.

I am therefore honoured to tell you that my own steps and style come directly from his influence because my teacher, Joy Adams, previously mentioned, was a student of his in London in the 1960s! My own observations of Gene Kelly, Fred Astaire and Sammy Davis Jr in their films, and my own imagination with music, added to this wonderful influence, begun so many years ago in 1920s America by Buddy.

To see these three famous dancers – Kelly, the Irishman with his tough and rooted traditional dance culture; Astaire, the European with his fabulous carriage and purpose; Sammy Davis Jr, with the obvious link to earth-bound rhythm and sound – is to see three different kinds of weight distribution: one air bound (Astaire), one earth bound (Sammy D.), and one (Kelly) using both. And that is where I am – light, but grounded.

As I said, basics tend to be basics. But I will try to get you to see things my way because I have had such a varied influence from many sources. What I will not do is admit that 'tap is just tap' and that there is only one way to do it. You could not say that jazz is just jazz; but you might agree that the waltz is the waltz, for most people. Only after learning the basics can you go on and develop things, through specialist teachers. But with the style I am giving you in this book, at the basic levels there are differences to note between those formalized ways and a more free way.

I guess I teach in class the way I learnt myself – from the person and not the page. It's how they used to learn tap in America and it's all right with me. How ironic and challenging that I am now trying to do that which I always resisted when I was learning! Oh well, it will teach me to dissent, eh?

So, I will go on to explain from here onwards:

- Where the weight should be and how to distribute for maximum effect.

- Why to be wholly on one foot matters because if you're not, you cannot move the other one.

- How to obey your brain's commands, because this small fact isn't as easy as it sounds.

- How to begin to bring all of this together in a series of structured Warm-Ups.

- How to: listen, assimilate, repeat to yourself, and put into practice that which is in your head.

For it must first be in your head, because it will never get to your feet if it is not! The brain has the 'map' along which the feet follow. It really is about listening to the beat and singing it to yourself and propelling your feet to the sound in your head.

The method I use a great deal here is the one where we literally take the main melody line or, if it is a song, the main lyric line.

We will tap our feet *only to that rhythm*. What I am aiming for here is to get you to move to *exactly* the sound of that melody line rhythm. The melody line is the one you sing when you recognize and hum the tune of a song you know.

It could be almost anything in the world of music. And from any period, for that matter. By singing to yourself you are connecting with the sound and, once connected, you can then move your feet. To tap only the sound of this rhythm is the aim. You will be doing the literal translation of repeating yourself! So you will be connecting your brain to your feet. Which, if you think about it, is one of *the* points of this book.

04 abbreviations and definitions

In this chapter you will learn:

- the abbreviations used in this book
- some terminology.

Abbreviations

Right foot (R)

Left foot (L)

Accented sound (a5)

Even link (and 5)

Flat (flt)

Step (stp) Step-heel (stp-hl) (espec. in combination)

Drop (drp)

Spring (spr)

Toe (to)

Hop (hp) Hop-step (hp-stp)

Ball-change (bl-ch)

Heel-ball (hl-bl) Ball-heel (bl-hl)

Brush (br) Heel-brush (hl-br)

Shuffle (shfl) Shuffle-step (shfl-stp)

Spring-point (spr-pt) Shuffle spring-point (shfl spr-pt)

Tap-step (tp-stp) Flap (flp)

Shuffle ball-change (shfl bl-ch)

Shuffle step-heel (shfl stp-hl)

Paddle (pdl) Four-beat paddle (4bt pdl)

Riff (rf) Three-beat riff (3bt rf)

Pick-up (p-up) Pick-up ball (p-up bl) Pick-up step (p-up stp)

Paddle-step (pdl-stp) Paddle step-heel (pdl stp-hl)

Shuffle step-heel point (shfl stp-hl pt)

Shuffle step-heel flat (shfl stp-hl flt)

Paddle step-heel point (pdl stp-hl pt)

Paddle step-heel flat (pdl stp-hl flt)

Tap-spring (tp-spr)

Stamp (stamp) stomp (stomp)

Four-beat cramp roll (4bt crmp rl)

Double pull-back (dbl pl-bk)

Shunt (always forward) (shnt)

Backward; forward (bkwd; fwd)

Definitions

Tap: a lifted beat, made with the toe, the heel or toe tip.

Beat: a non-lifted tap – a strike with the toe or heel that remains in contact with the floor after the action.

Step: a change of weight; going from the L to the R or vice versa. Can also mean a short collection of elements, e.g. shfl bl-ch.

Hop: a change of weight from one foot to the same foot.

Spring: a change of weight from one foot to the other with energy and purpose.

Drop: a change of weight from one foot to the other onto a flat foot, with energy and purpose.

Ball-change: a very quick double change of weight, back to the original foot. Does not have to be ball of foot, can change to flat foot. Principle applies to any step with this weight change, and in any direction.

Pick-up: one sound, with toe lifted and heel in contact, made with the toe tap 'picking up' and backwards and striking the floor on the way.

Pick-up step: two sounds, one with the toe tap, one with the landing on the ball of foot. Adding a heel will produce a **pick-up step heel**.

>>>: to the right.

<<<: to the left.

05 tempo, melody, rhythm

In this chapter you will learn:

- how to listen in
- how to bring it out.

Okay, just how do you put the sound in your head for the feet to follow?

Ever repeated a song in your head? Ever picked up a knife and fork and beat out a rhythm on a table (to the annoyance of others)? Ever heard your footsteps on a wooden floor and liked the sound? Ever played the drums in your head to a track on the radio? Or banged a plastic cup on a table just to hear the rhythm coming out of you? Great – you can probably tap dance too!

Track list

1 Melody 1

So find that tune now, in among the many tunes you have in your possession. It can be any one of a million songs – and from different artists. Try Frank Sinatra, George Gershwin, Cole Porter, Elton John, Billy Joel, the Beatles, Duke Ellington, Ella Fitzgerald, Queen or Harry Connick Jr, and don't forget Hip Hop! There must be a million Show tunes just for starters.

Find the tempo. Tempo means *time* and this is the measure of counts the tune is using. Now find the first count of the musical bar – the bar is a collection of the counts – (and hopefully this is obvious, because it's the strong or emphatic beat) and the last count of the bar (again obvious). Note how many of these beats there are

in the bar. If you find this difficult at first, try another tune until it becomes clearer.

So we have:

- counts – a collection of counts to a bar
- a collection of bars to a phrase
- a collection of phrases in a piece of music.

All in a tempo or measure. This is usually the same from the beginning to the end of the piece of music.

Jazz music is almost always in the 4/4 measure (4 quarter notes to a bar), so I hope you have at least one of these pieces of music in your collection! It would be unusual if not!

Now find the melody. It can be loosely called the tune or the song line itself; it's what makes the song singable, and in more traditional songs it is the piano that often leads the melody. Just as well the piano is a percussion instrument because that is what we are into here!

Now for the rhythm, which is absolutely linked to the melody. The melody is supported by the rhythm of the other instruments and in a band piece each instrument will be played perhaps with its own rhythm. This is called an arrangement and there will be a separate one for the saxophone, the drums, the guitar, the trumpet and the piano. Don't forget, the voice is also an instrument and this will have its own melody too.

Let us take an example from a well-known tune, *When I'm Sixty-Four*, by the Beatles. Fix it in your head; don't play the music. Hum it to yourself.

Depending on your age, situation and even culture, I will assume, for the purposes of example, you have heard of this song. It has a predictable and common melodic quality. If you can sing this song, or just 'la la la' it, you can move your feet to it.

When I'm Sixty-Four
When I get older, losing my hair …
Many years from now (de de-de de-deee)
Will you still be sending me a Valentine?
Birthday greetings, bottle of wine?

Or:

La la la la-la, la la la laaa
La laaa la la laaa (de de-de de-deee)

La la-la la-la la-la la-la la laaa
La la la la, la la-la laaa.

And to write it down:

If we imitate these sounds with our feet we have a good basis to tap dance. We are obeying our own 'head-map' and producing the sound that is already ours in our heads. Even using single beats on the balls of our feet, we can reproduce this melody. Next, we would produce a rhythm over the top of this melody, using basic tap dance steps written in this book. Listen to the CD for similar rhythms.

In Chapter 08, Rhythm and counting explained, I will explore this written concept more fully. But for now, to write down the counting of *When I'm Sixty-Four* is as in the four figures, with each circle representing a single *dancer's* bar of music and the numbers as the counts.

When reading this, begin counting with the empty dot and count always clockwise, only saying the filled in dot '●'.

Don't worry about this written concept; there will be more of this later. But for now just try it out for size.

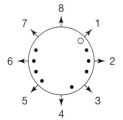

figure 5.1 When I get older, losing my hair

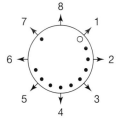

figure 5.3 Will you still be sending me a Valentine?

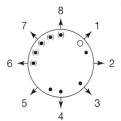

figure 5.2 Many years from now (de de-de de-deee)

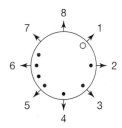

figure 5.4 Birthday greetings, bottle of wine?

06 warm-ups

In this chapter you will learn:

- how to stand
- how to connect your brain to your feet
- some basic warm-up exercises.

Warming up is easy to do and can look deceptively simple. Remember though, you are focusing on those parts of your legs and feet that will do a job of work. You must be in a warm space and hopefully with a wooden floor under your feet. If this is not possible, a hard floor of some kind will be fine. A carpeted floor sort of defeats the object of tap dancing anyway, so I will assume you have either a hard floor surface or a board laid flat on carpet. A board is a great practice aid anyway and you should, as I mentioned, ideally buy one. I will also assume you are wearing tap shoes or hard leather-soled shoes that will make a sound you can hear. No rubber-soled shoes from now on!

You can use music here or not. It would, however, benefit you to use something – and something you think you would like to dance to once you have learned a few elements. Perhaps a favourite piece or the pieces included on the CD. If you are to use music, you must start practising from now to keep in time – to keep with the tempo.

Tap dancing at this stage is mostly about the knees and feet. The hips are also used, but less, for example, than in ballroom dancing. At the same time attention must be paid to the body and the arms, which will play a part in later stages. The co-ordination of toes, heels, stamps, brushes, knees and the brain will be our focus here!

Track list

2 Warm-up 1

3 Warm-up 2

4 Warm-up 3

Warm-up 1

> **Always:**
>
> The shoulders, hips, head and neck are relaxed, the weight is forward; the knees are flexing; the heels are down for now; the arms are under light tension and not just hanging; the mid torso is under light tension and not slumped (picture 6.1).

1. Stand with feet about shoulder width apart, slightly turned out only, and bounce and straighten in the knees, both knees at once. *No sound* in the feet. Do this for 16 counts (picture 6.2).

picture 6.2 Bounce and straighten

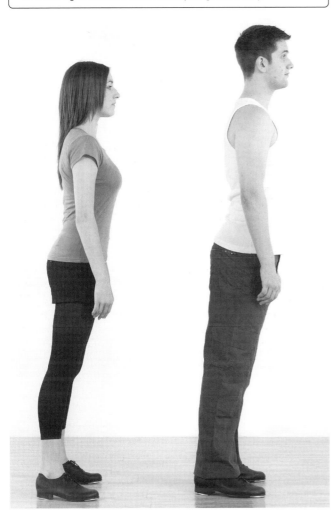

picure 6.1 Always ...

2. Step (stp) into each foot, on the ball of foot, and flex and stretch in each knee, in a 'walking' action (picture 6.3). *No sound* in the feet, just a weight transfer from left to right. Do this for 16 counts.

4. Step into each foot, on the ball, and this time *do* stay in a bent-leg position and increase the weight into each foot (step heavier). Keep time for 16 counts and beat the sound into the floor.

picture 6.3 Stepping

picture 6.4 Springing

3. Step into each foot, on the ball of foot, and flex and stretch in each knee. Do not stay in a bent-leg position, but rather use bending *and* straightening. *Sound* the feet this time, using the ball of foot (but of course, the toe tap will sound too.)

5. Spring (spr) into each foot, from one to the other, with a light landing each time in each foot, and of course on the ball (picture 6.4). Knees should be raised in the front and not with feet picking up behind. Feet remain under you. Do this for 16 counts, or more if you want to.

All we have done here is transfer weight. We have also tried to find where our weight is – forward and not back, or upright; down, but not heavy into the floor; and up lightly on the balls of feet. Hopefully you have found the middle way, which is where I want you to be.

With a basic rhythm

Now we can elaborate this easy warm-up with a basic rhythm. If you can do this part, you have already begun to tap dance.

1. Stand with feet about shoulder width apart, slightly turned out only.

2. Step, beginning R and with *sound* and *weight*, the following rhythm (don't forget – the balls of your feet!):

No music ... count ...

R L R   L R L   R   L   R L R L

1 2 3 __ 5 6 7 __ 1 __ 3 __ a5 6 7 __

Step on the numbers only, and pause on the spaces.

This is basic timing, pausing and transference. Here is another:

Use CD track 2.

R   L   R L R L   R L R L R L

1 __ 3 __ a5 6 7 __ a1 2 3 4 5 __ __ __

As you can see, I have included 'a5' and 'a1'. This is a very close link of two sounds – an *accented* sound – and is closer than an *even* link which would be 'and 5' or 'and 1'. In this particular instance this accented step is called a ball-change (bl-ch). See Chapter 07 Steps and sounds.

picture 6.5   Spring heavier

6. Spring into each foot, from one to the other, but with a heavier landing each time in each foot, and of course, again on the ball (picture 6.5). Knees should be raised in the front and not with feet picking up behind. Feet remain under you as before. Do this for as many as you want to.

All transfers are logical, in other words a complete weight change every time a step is taken. You should slightly lift the other foot when transferring to be certain you are 100 per cent committed into the transfer of weight. Try one more:

Use CD track 3.

R L RL R   L R
1 2 a3 4 __ 6 7 __

Repeat on the other side.

If you do this correctly, with the pauses in place, you should recognize this famous syncopation.

> **Remember:**
> - Weight transfer is exactly that – a complete 100 per cent transfer from foot to foot. A point often missed.
> - Do not add a single extra sound! 12 sounds are 12.
> - Keep the weight forward – no flat-footed landings.
> - Keep time – exercise your brain as you go along.

> **Major point:**
>
> **Trap** The rhythm in your head.
>
> **Clap** The rhythm in your hands.
>
> **Tap** The rhythm in your feet.

At this point, we can see that we have a basic rhythm counting method and a basic set of warm-up exercises. We then have to bring the two strands together by expanding the simple warm-up and putting it to a rhythm. The following is a sort of beginning to everything we shall attempt:

Listen to the sound of the music track; listen for the time, melody and rhythm – and dance or sound (or copy) exactly what you hear.

After this, the logical follow-on is that we make up a very simple rhythm *around* this given rhythm.

And that is tap dance – listening for ways to use our own rhythm *over the rhythm* already in the music. Then we become another instrument, along with those we are hearing.

Warm-up 2

Use CD track 3 for this exercise. It involves balance and co-ordination.

> **Major point:**
>
> *Your* balance is *your* problem! Practise your balance everywhere you can. Wait for the train … on one foot; make the tea … on one foot; pour the drink standing on one leg; answer the telephone standing on one leg. The other foot just has to be imperceptibly lifted off the ground. This is good practice and costs nothing.

We balance using many muscles, from the larger leg groups to the back and stomach muscles. I have already mentioned that the torso must be under tension (for any dance discipline) but don't forget the buttocks! Use all of these muscle groups to gain control of your own balance. I usually start every beginners' class by asking people to stand with a feeling of the weight being forward, i.e. sloping slightly forward. This will lift the heels off the floor slightly but you are not on your toes. I use the expression 'You are not on your toes; it's just that your heels are not quite on the floor'. When you are standing, of course you feel you are flat, but keep the weight forward idea in mind.

> **Always:**
>
> The shoulders, hips, head and neck are relaxed, the weight is forward; the knees are flexed and held in one position; the arms are under slight tension; the mid torso is under light tension and not slumped.

Do the basic Warm-up 1 and then do these flexes and circles:

1. Balance with weight in the L, knee slightly bent, foot flat. In the mirror, see the R leg in front and slightly to the side, knee bent and with the end of the toe tap on the floor, heel lifted.

   (The leg we stand on is called the *supporting* leg and the other is the *working* leg.)

2. Keeping the R leg still, *raise then point* the toe of the R, with a sound on the floor from the toe tap, as hard as possible, to build strength in a small movement.

picture 6.6a   Ankle flex up

picture 6.6b   Ankle flex down with force

You are using the flexor muscle in the shin and the extensor muscle in the calf. *Tap* the floor, using only the ankle movement. Bring the toe up off the floor in a quick action (pictures 6.6a and b).

Do this for 16 counts on each side.

Add to this next by beating the floor (momentarily keeping the toe down).

picture 6.7a   Balance before flexing

Major point:

The ankles in tap dance are almost never relaxed. If they were, the foot would be no more effective than a fish on the end of your leg, flopping and flipping. The actual foot itself is relaxed – toe to heel – but the ankle is fully engaged for the whole time.

Do the above exercise for 15 counts, because you must transfer on the sixteenth count to the other side, if we are to maintain our 'brain train' idea.

Then do it again for:

● 7 counts, changing on 8

● 3 counts, changing on 4

● 1 count, changing on 2.

Don't forget to fully flex! Listen for bar endings.

picture 6.7b   Ankle flex up to the side

This will help to build up strength in a very small part of the body, but very important for our use here. We are trying to gain the maximum from the minimum, so to speak.

You can do it all again, but this time with foot out to the side (pictures 6.7a and b).

1. In circling, use the same beginning, i.e. standing on balance, with one foot forward, in front but lifted and flexed; to the same counts each side, circle fully the foot from the ankle. Really isolate the ankle from the leg, and indeed, keep the legs bent and still – one supporting and one working.

2. Circle clockwise for 15 and change on 16 to circle the L; repeat circling anticlockwise for 15 and change. Go on for the rest of the counting, next using 7 counts and so on. Take the foot to the side and repeat all again.

3. You can do all of this again but striking the floor as you circle.

As when slicing bread each hand has a specific job to do, rather like the legs do here. But attempt to work one without the other and the job does not get done.

Warm-up 3

This warm-up incorporates isolation, co-ordination, balance and strength. Use CD track 4.

1. Stand on L, knees bent, with R toe resting beside. Remembering to fully flex each ankle every time, beat the toe tap into the floor with maximum force, but also lift it up again immediately afterwards.

2. Now, take the R foot to the side over 3 beats, e.g. 1,2,3>>>; and 1 2 3 <<<. Do this with the intention of using the calf muscle and flexor muscles to maximum effect, trying to get as much power into a tiny movement as possible. It is rather like a one-inch punch. (The martial arts legend Bruce Lee was credited with developing a one-inch punch to propel a person right across a room, by means of this short and very sharp action!)

3. As you do this 8 times, count it so ... out, in; out ... in and so on, for both the R and the L.

After this, do the same to the front and to the back using the same counts. The backward exercise would actually go as far behind as your leg can go and with a turned out ankle; but throughout all of this the leg itself does not help the beating action.

Isolate the ankle so that only the foot moves to do the beat; the leg merely takes the foot either out or in ... or forward or back.

Now, do the same counting but do the following pattern:

R>>>1 2 3; <<<1 2 3; >>>1 2 3; <<<1 2 3;

Fwd 1 2 3; bkwd to behind 1 2 3; round to right side 1 2 3; <<<1 2 3.

Close R to L at the end and repeat all on the L side.

07 steps and sounds

In this chapter you will learn:

- basic sounds
- basic elements
- basic construction.

Steps one two three ... as easy as abc

The predominant single sound you use will be a step (stp), as covered in Chapter 06 Warm-ups. In Chapter 08 Rhythm and counting explained you will see how this single sound can be used to produce various rhythms. We will also use others: the spring (spr) (really a step but with more energy and elevation), the toe (to), the hop (hp) and the heel (hl).

Track list

5	Shuffles 123	**17**	Shuffles sound
6	Ball Heel 123		
7	Shuffle Step 123	**18**	Shuffle Step sound
8	Shuffle Step Heel 123	**19**	Shuffle Step Heel sound
20	Paddles sound		
21	Paddle Step sound		
22	Paddle Step Heel sound		
23	3 Beat Paddle sound		
24	Paddle Step In Triplet sound		

Another single sound is the brush (br) (a forward or backward action using the toe tap to strike or 'brush' the floor) and this is included below.

Shuffle (shfl)

The shuffle is fundamental to tap dancing and is constantly used. Get it right now and it will be with you forever.

It is the first double sounding, or two-beat sound. This is a very important and essential thing to learn. The sound here will be:

'a1 a2 a3...' CD track 5 gives a good example of this warm-up rhythm. Also listen to CD track 17.

1. Stand, balancing on the L, knee slightly bent and with the R in front. The toe tap is in contact with the floor and the heel is lifted, leg is bent (picture 7.1a).

2. Lift the R, and using the ankle as much as you can, brush (br) the toe tap forward and backward, *with sound on contacting the floor* (pictures 7.1b–e).

picture 7.1a   Stand in balance

picture 7.1b   Forward brush contact

picture 7.1c   After contact

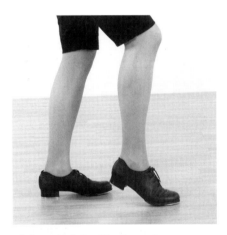 

picture 7.1d   On the return contact

picture 7.1e   After contact

3. Flex the foot every time you brush, so that the forward tap is up and lifted and the backward tap is also up and lifted. Do not point the toe to the floor; you are brushing the tap and tapping the sound, so it must not feel sticky or heavy along the floor.

The knee must lift every time, but always in front. At no time does the foot swing behind you. Don't forget, the rhythm is 'a1 a2 a3' (br-br, br-br, br-br).

4. Do this 15 times and change on the sixteenth to the other side. But *land on the ball of foot.* Flat-footed landings are not allowed. See below for more of this.

Style point:

Some styles will advocate the foot coming behind on the backward brush. This is not like that here, because this is more of an American style in execution and not European. Lift the knee, flex the foot; lift the knee, flex the foot and keep the leg and foot in front.

5. Then continue for 7 counts, change on '8'; 3 counts, change on '4'; 1 count, change on '2'. You will end by combining into the next logical step, a shuffle-step (shfl-stp), which happens to be our first *triple sounding* step!

But first, you can do all of the above again but with the foot shuffling out to the side (pictures 7.2a and b).

6. Count it so, for the '7' change on '8':

a1 a2 a3 a4 a5 a6 a7 8	R
a1 a2 a3 a4 a5 a6 a7 8	L
then: a1 a2 a3 4	R
a5 a6 a7 8	L

then:

a1 2 R	(shuffle-step)
a3 4 L	(")
a5 6 R	(")
a7 8 L	(")

picture 7.2a   The shuffle – brush forward

picture 7.2b   The shuffle – brush backwards

Shuffle-step (shfl-stp)

This last one – shuffle 1, change on 2 – automatically gives us a shuffle-step and as a separate exercise is still counted:

then:	a1 2	R	(shuffle-step)
	a3 4	L	(")
	a5 6	R	(")
	a7 8	L	(")

> **Major point:**
>
> On landing, stepping from one foot to the other, land with a dynamic step and not just using gravity. Be positive about it because this down action will free the other foot faster to do the exercise on the other side.

Change weight always through ball of foot, lowering the rest of the foot afterwards if it has to end flat. You need to hear only the ball strike the floor. The heel will follow and this will lead to the foot becoming flat but now with a controlled sound. The alternative is to stay on the ball, and this is not practical in this exercise.

You can do all of this again but with the foot shuffling out to the side instead of the front. Try the step with track 7 of the CD. Follow the rhythm changes. Also listen to CD track 18.

This side position is more a jazz line and adds, I think, a more relaxed and free approach, especially as in the mirror, you can see both feet and a good leg line. You should just be able to see both of the heels, but do not turn out too much on either leg. Both legs are still bent, shuffles both lifted and flexed. Do not stand in parallel position or pigeon-toed – you will fail every audition!

Spring-point (spr-pt)

Stand with weight forward, arms and mid torso under light tension. Balance on the L, but with the R out to side, toe in contact with floor.

picture 7.3   Good balance (for spring-point)

Feel like you are completely in balance on your left side. Foot is flat, knee is slightly bent, hip is held, chest over hip, head over the front of the L (look down and check!); take the R off the floor and now you know if you are in balance. Re-contact the R toe on the floor (picture 7.3).

Spring from one foot to the other, sounding both feet – one will land on the ball of foot only, the other will sound only the toe tap, out to the side (pictures 7.4a–d). Keep your weight forward. Go through a **centre line**, bringing the R into the L, then the L out to the side.

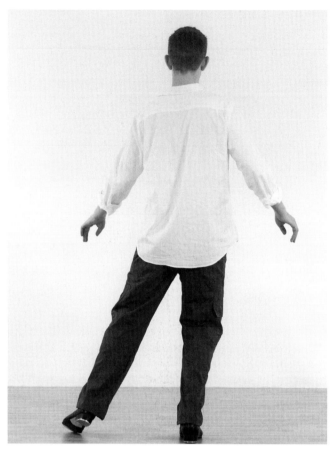

picture 7.4a   Spring-point from left to right …

picture 7.4b   … going through …

Major point:

The Centre – what is it? Actually, it is **two** things in dance.

You must go through an imaginary centre line. If you think of a pendulum arm, it goes through a centre line, and the arm swings through it equally. *You must equalize your body also.*

Look down through the **centre line** and between your feet and imagine a spot on the floor, or mark the floor.

The centre is also that part of the body called the mid torso and is a great controlling feature of any dancing activity.

When you spring here your legs and feet go through this centre spot, and it should feel rather like one foot is pushing the other out of the way in order to take its place on the floor.

Stay grounded here. Do not spring up, but use your spring to land down, and with a positive sound.

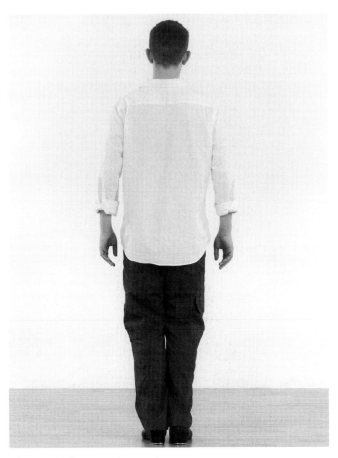

picture 7.4c   ... the centre ...

picture 7.4d   ... to the other side.

Style point:

Spring down and not up. Think of a car and its springs – it does not go any higher than it is made to be off the ground. *But* the springs allow it to go lower and back to its position. So it springs down. We have this natural spring too.

Major point:

'a1 a2 a3' and so on. This is a basic accented sound and is found everywhere in tap dance. For example: shuffle, ball-change, hop-step, ball-heel, tap-step.

It's sort of a heartbeat, too ... d dub; d dub; d dub. See Chapter 08 Rhythm and counting explained.

Okay, count it so:

RL   LR   RL   LR   RL   LR   RL   LR

a1   a2   a3   a4   a5   a6   a7   a8

This is the same sound as that for the shuffle.

Ball heel (bl-hl)

This can also be called step-heel, especially within combinations. Listen to track 6 of the CD.

1. Step deeply onto the *ball* of foot, beat the *heel* afterwards. No gravity here ... use a separate and firm pressure action for each sound, as if going into the floor. The ball is very important, because it is your point of contact every time you transfer weight! And it is a little like walking downstairs – the ball lands first and the heel follows. Except that here we need to *sound* it!

Ball change (bl-ch)

1. Stand in the L, do a ball into the floor with the R, taking the weight out of the L, landing behind the L foot. Now change your weight back into the L with a step. You will make two sounds here. But ... a ball-change can be anywhere. A ball-change is a ball-change is a ball-change! Not just 'back-front', in other words. But here yes, to practise.

Also, the change can be into a ball or into a flat foot, depending on what is required next. The action of doing a ball and a change of weight is in principle, the same in all cases.

There will be more 'letters' later in the book.

We will now combine our 'abc' steps to give us short 'words'.

Shuffle spring-point (shfl spr-pt)

1. Do a single shuffle to the side and spring onto the foot that does it, touching the other foot to the side on the point of the tap (inside edge, as it lands). The weight obviously remains on the ball of the springing foot.

Count it so:

shfl	spr-pt	shfl	spr-pt	shfl	spr-pt	shfl	spr-pt
R	R – L	L	L – R	R	R – L	L	L – R
a1	a2	a3	a4	a5	a6	a7	a8

This is springing on both sides. Have patience here ... it's a big leap forward!

Remember:

Trap, **Clap**, **Tap** the rhythm in your head, hands, feet.

picture 7.5a Brush forward

picture 7.5b Brush backward

picture 7.5c Land on the ball

Shuffle step-heel (shfl stp-hl)

Do likewise with this next step. Shuffle again to the side, step on the ball of the same foot, and beat the heel of the same foot (pictures 7.5a–d).

Count it so:

```
shfl  stp-hl   shfl  stp-hl   shfl  stp-hl   shfl  stp-hl
       R         L             R             L
a1     a2    a3   a4    a5    a6   a7    a8
```

Go through your centre. Transfer completely. Do exactly the feet sounds – a clear, lifted shuffle, a positive landing in the centre on the ball of foot, a positive beat, completing the transfer of weight, on the heel.

Now try this step to track 8 of the CD. Also listen to CD track 19.

picture 7.5d Heel beat

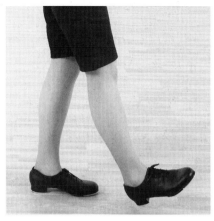

picture 7.6a Brush forward

picture 7.6b Brush backward (to complete the shuffle)

picture 7.6c Ball

picture 7.6d Change

Shuffle-ball change (shfl bl-ch)

Use CD track 8.

1. Stand in the L, ready as before but shuffle to the front, put down the ball behind the L, change into a flat foot on the L, with knees bent. Try now to shuffle to the side and put down the ball beside the L and change into a ball on the L (pictures 7.6a–d).

I hope you can see the versatility of this sweet step; we can make a lot of use of it.

> **Remember:**
>
> Trap, Clap, Tap … you should be getting the idea by now!

The paddle

I am grateful to the paddle to this day, because it is no less than *the* basic step of Rhythm Tap itself – a step used by all of the great dancers in the movies of old and by those dancers who were not known but who were sometimes equally as gifted. This one step is the staple of the whole style of close-work tap dancing and among tappers the world over, the step of choice for speed, clarity, versatility and invention.

The paddle is two sounds and is very like the shuffle … strike one sound with a forward action, strike two with a backward action. It has the same uses, but because it is much closer to the floor, can be many times faster than the shuffle. It simply takes less time to execute the two sounds; it uses less movement in the ankle and knee, therefore it can be speeded up to sometimes fantastic speeds.

Use CD track 20.

1. Stand in the L foot, R ready to go, with the foot flat. Doing this in slow motion, think of 'peeling' the heel of the R off the floor, toe remaining in contact (picture 7.7a). The knee is slowly flexing and this will peel the heel from the floor. Keep this going until the whole foot lifts from the floor and then use the natural straightening of the knee to bring the rear edge of the heel down in a 'digging' action to the floor where it naturally falls (picture 7.7b). Do not brush the heel; it must stop on the floor where it lands.

picture 7.7a   Peel the heel

picture 7.7b   Dig the heel

picture 7.7c   Pick-up contact

picture 7.7d   Pick-up backward

2. Bend the knee again to reverse this action and pull the toe tap back and upwards, striking the floor in a 'picking up' action – a pick-up (p-up) (pictures 7.7c and d). We can call this two sound step a 'heel pick-up', or a 'heel dig and pick-up' ... or we can call it what it has always been called – a paddle. Try a few repeats of this on the counts as for shuffles, i.e. 'a1, a2, a3, a4, a5' and so on.

Don't try to help the action by moving in the ankle at all; in fact keep the ankle very still and use the knee action only. The ankle is in a permanent flex.

Putting the foot down in the ball only will give us three sounds and we can use similar terms for the earlier shuffle-step – a paddle-step (pdl-stp). Putting the heel down now in addition will give us four sounds and again we can use similar references to the shuffle step-heel and say paddle step-heel (pdl stp-hl). I will refer to these two things as a '3 beat paddle' and a '4 beat paddle' as we progress. They can be done to the front or side (picture 7.8).

picture 7.8   Paddling to front and side

Now try to do multiples of these.

1. Stand on the L and lift the R heel as before, bring the heel forward to strike the floor, reverse the action and do a pick-up with the toe, landing the ball on the floor and then the heel. Remember to change weight into the ball and heel in order to do the same on the other foot. Relax as you do this and the speed will naturally increase. Go from foot to foot and achieve a fluid transfer of weight from one side to the other (pictures 7.9a–d).

Count it so:

For paddles: 'a1, a2, a3, a4, a5, a6, a7, a8' on one side only. CD track 20.

For paddle-step: 'and a 1; and a 2; and a 3; and a 4', and so on. CD tracks 21, 23 and 24.

For paddle step-heel: 'and and a 1; and and a 2; and and a 3', etc. CD track 22. As you can perhaps see, the same imperial measures are there in this step in the form of: accented eighth notes, twelfth notes and sixteenth notes.

picture 7.9a   Heel

picture 7.9b   Pull

picture 7.9c   Ball

picture 7.9d   Heel

Sounds one two three ... as easy as do re mi

Now, we have arrived at the point where we are combining the sounds with the steps. The basic principle of adding up the sounds and steps by doing something extra, thereby making something new (e.g. a shuffle becomes a shuffle-step as soon as we put that foot on the floor, and then that becomes a shuffle step-heel as soon as we put the heel down) is explained as follows:

1. Stepping from one foot to the other, within a tempo, on the ball of foot, knees and feet lifted to the front. Then, with a rhythm to make it more interesting.

2. Linking two sounds, and not two separate sounds, will give us a basic rhythm structure, written as: 'a1, a2, a3, a4', etc.

   The shuffle is the prime example; the ball-heel is another; the spring-point is another, and the paddle, of course.

3. Linking three sounds, not three separate sounds, will give us another basic rhythm signature and can be written in more than one way. We have written it in our shuffle step exercise as: 'a1 2; a3 4; a5 6; a7 8'. But it could also be: 'and a 1; and a 2; and a 3; and a 4' or even '1 and a; 2 and a; 3 and a; 4 and a'. The paddle-step is ideal for this last example. Listen to CD track 24.

So, really the logical follow-on is that we can go on producing these linked pieces in increasing numbers of sounds, and we have already done four examples – the shuffle step-heel (shfl stp-hl), shuffle spring-point (shfl spr-pt), shuffle ball-change (shfl bl-ch), paddle step-heel (pdl stp-hl). It is a good idea to try these four steps to this one rhythm, written here: 'a1 a2; a3 a4; a5 a6; a7 a8'. We have a four-beat linked sound.

How about a further example, which I will call ball-heel ball-heel (bl-hl, bl-hl). The rhythm for this lovely step can be either *even* or *accented* – 'and 1 and 2; a1 a2' – and you can practise it for the 'great speed with little effort' I talked about at the beginning!

Remember, these are linked sounds.

It again follows that we can go on doing this, by adding another sound, and making that a five-beat sounding step, another one and we have a six-beat sounding step, and so on. Try these out:

Shuffle step-heel point (shfl stp-hl pt)

1. Stand on the L, R out to side. Shfl R, bringing the leg in towards your centre line and land it down firmly on the ball. Begin to change weight now, as the R heel comes down. At this point exactly you have completely transferred into the R side.

2. Lift the L off the floor and land the point of the toe (inside edge of toe tap) on the floor to the L side. This is five sounds (linked five sounds) and can now be called a shfl stp-hl pt.

3. If you put the L foot flat, and perform a heavy full-foot sound, with or without weight, we can call it a shuffle step-heel flat (shfl stp-hl flt). This is a good finishing sound at the end of a phrase or bar, and it counts so: 'a1 and a 2' (picture 7.10).

You will like the sound of these two using the much faster paddle in place of the shuffle – paddle step-heel point (pdl stp-hl pt) and paddle step-heel flat (pdl stp-hl flt).

picture 7.10   Finish with style!

08 rhythm and counting explained

In this chapter you will learn:

- how to count
- how to visualize rhythm
- how to use a Rhythm Clock.

More or less everything in life has rhythm. Buildings have rhythm, flowers have rhythm, engines have rhythm, *we* have rhythm. And in dance we *need* rhythm. In this case, Western centric rhythm.

In some Eastern countries, such as Vietnam, Tibet, Outer Mongolia, the rhythm structures can vary so widely as to be hard to understand in our part of the world, especially if it is their traditional musical form. In the West we have a rhythm structure based on a format called 'strict tempo'. This is decided by a regular spacing of counts that we usually divide up into sections, called bars.

Then we decide on a 'feel' or way with the tempo, and come up with '3/4' or '2/4' or '4/4' or '6/8' – 3 beats to a bar, 2 beats to a bar, 4 beats – and there are more, complicated further as the divides become either mixed or irregular. So, a piece of music could be written using all of the above and even more. The most common is 4/4 but the waltz, for instance, is in 3/4, the tango is 2/4. Jazz music in the main is 4/4 and it is easy to identify this when listening and counting to music of the 'swing era' or before.

Great musicians such as Count Basie, Duke Ellington, Irving Berlin and George Gershwin all used more than one signature, but it's a safe bet that most of their jazz compositions were in 4/4. This is to say we count four beats to a bar and the bars are written in quarter notes. By dividing it up we can keep a watchful eye on it and everyone reads the same thing the same way. Thus, we have sheet music that is in the global lexicon and the people of the world all read from the same standpoint.

So, let's try to *visualize* the counting we need in tap dancing.

We will use a 4/4 and imagine the beats in a line from left to right. A good analogy is to picture an ordinary ruler where the divisions are clearly spaced and marked. You can read centimetres and millimetres and if it was long enough, a full metre. In the old rulers the divides were even more fine – a foot, an inch, a half-inch, a quarter, an eighth, a twelfth and even a sixteenth! An *imperial* measure!

And in fact that is how we can do our counting here.

8...1...2...3...4...5...6...7...8...1...2...
   (..............V... ....)

Above, the dance bar is between (and) and the counts to divide it are from one to eight, which is two fours. We call the tempo in quarter notes and there are four of them in each bar. As dancers we use eight quarter notes in our bars because there are two fours in our bars.

Now, a dancer counts in 8s because it is easier for the body to handle, and also it is traditional; an American (and thus an imperial) way of counting dance, which often annoys musicians who, of course, count in 4s by tradition. We will deal in 8s only. (You may have heard the expression '5, 6, 7, 8 !' in a dance film or video and certainly in a dance studio.)

So, this is our measure around which we can construct our rhythm. If we tapped to the tempo alone we would be just following the beat; and there is nothing wrong with that. Except to say it could become quite boring in a few moments!

Let us take the space between 1 and 2 ... and then begin dividing thus:

1...2   1/4th

1.....................and.................2   1/8th

1...............and...............a.......2   1/12th

1.........and...........and..........a.....2   1/16th

The first line we can say is our tempo and we count it in quarter notes; this is *one* quarter-note measure.

So, as we divide down we will get equal measures – the next line is thus in eighth notes, the next is in twelfth notes and the next line is in sixteenth notes.

Remember our old ruler? Our imperial ruler?

BUT, there is just one more we need to know:

1..a.............2 acc 1/8th

These are the very important accented eighth notes and in fact you have already done this rhythm in the shuffle ball-change and the ball-heel, ball-heel earlier.

I have given some examples of counting and syncopation on tracks **9** and **10** of the CD.

Syncopation will give us rhythm. Loosely explained, syncopation is often the tune or melody line, the bit that leads the song or piece of music. The bass guitar may be just keeping tempo, the drums also. But the clarinet or piano will be syncopating, producing what we know as the tune.

Let's take the tune *I Got Rhythm* by George Gershwin. Below on the first line are the 8 counting *beats* in the bar, on the second line is the actual way we should count the *rhythm*, with the *lyrics* below that.

1 2 3 4 5 6 7 8 1 2 3 4 5 6 7 8

  • • • •   • • • •

  I got rhy thm;   I got mus ic

The point of this is that such a simple little tune as *I Got Rhythm* is not simply 1 2 3 4. It is actually using the beat and the spaces in between. These spaces in between have to be identified and are the 'and' or the 'a' as mentioned above.

So, this rhythm is spoken as: (1) 2 (3) and (4) 5 (6) and (7) (8).

In this book, rhythm will be written thus:

__ 2 __ and __ 5 __ and __ __

Listen carefully to track 10 on the CD. The '1, 3, 4, 6, 7, 8' are not used at all! This missing out will give us syncopation. By omitting counts we are implying a stress on the ones that remain, but we need to keep track of them. The space will look like an underline, thus: __.

Pretty much every tune can be notated this way, but who wants to do that? Far too hard; leave it to the teachers, eh?

But we do have to know about it and I believe it is fascinating to be able to count. This new vocabulary called tap dancing has to have a kind of grammar.

The Rhythm Clock

A new and, until now, completely unknown way to visualize rhythm follows below. My own method is arranged in a circle. You may find this visually more interesting. The circle is the bar, and the • are the actual way to count the rhythm.

Example 1 I Got Rhythm

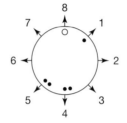

Use CD track 11.

Read clockwise.

Begin with ○ always

Only say the ○ and •

I got rhy...thm

figure 8.1

Example 2 Anything Goes

Use CD track 12.

Only say the ○ and •

First line of the song:

a1 2 3 4 5 6 and __ a8

In olden days a glimpse
Of stocking was

figure 8.2

Example 3 Singin' in the Rain

This is how to count the first line of the song:

8 1.......a4 a5.......

I'm s-i-n-g in' in the rain

where 1,2,3,6,7 are held or sustained notes

figure 8.3

This short exercise can be performed to the tune from *I Got Rhythm*. Use CD track 11.

I got rhythm

stp	stp	stp	bl-ch	stp
R	L	R	L-R	L
__ 2 __	and	__ 5 __	a7	8

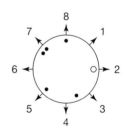

figure 8.4

I got music

stp	stp	stp	stp	bl-ch	stp
R	L	R	L	R-L	R
1	2 ___	and ___	5 ___	a7	8

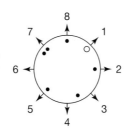

figure 8.5

I got my gal

stp	stp	stp	stp	bl-ch
L	R	L	R	L-R
1	2 ___	and ___	5 ___	a7

figure 8.6

Who could ask for anything more?

shfl-stp	stp	shfl-stp	stp
L	R	L	R
8 and 1	2	3 and 4	5 ___ ___

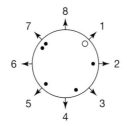

figure 8.7

This all reads as follows:

Step, step, step, ball-change, step step (2 times).

then:

Step, step, step, ball-change

and the Break:

Shuffle-step step, shuffle-step step.

Obviously we have danced around the sparse four beats identified above. But that's what your instrument is for! To embellish at will; to find your own way with your new 'voice' – your tapping feet. Now, keep in mind the tune and make up another piece with the same sort of basic moves. You will be surprised at how quickly you get the idea.

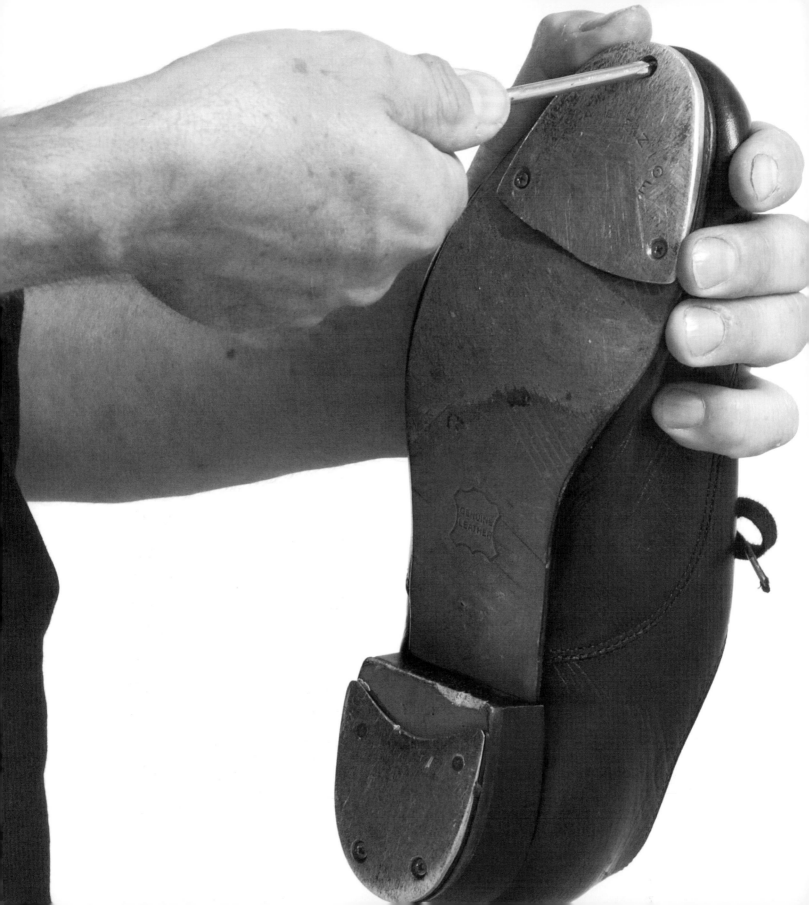

09 building blocks – basic vocabulary

In this chapter you will learn:

- to begin linking steps and building a routine
- more about syncopation
- some more great steps.

Tap dance is a bit of a numbers game I sometimes think – we use numbers to add to numbers to create other numbers that are then different from the original numbers! So, 123 consists of 1 and 2 and 3, but also 12, 13, 23, 32, 21, 31, 321, 231, 132 – it is merely the rearranging of them that make the results so different.

Track list

12 Melody 3

13 Melody 4

14 Melody 5

15 Melody 6

16 Melody 7

This addition system works here, but with letters in place of numbers. We have made a basic set and we have the beginnings of a kind of a vocabulary. I want to use the same principle of rearrangement to create new things but still retain the pure set of items we have.

We have to master the 'abc of it, to get to the xyz of it', as Sammy Cahn might have meant in his great song, *Teach Me Tonight*. So, c - a - t spells 'cat' and b - a - t spells 'bat'. But first we have to recognize a b c and t.

I am trying, then, to give your mind a process of assimilation, partly because it is a challenge to get across by book what is obviously a sound-based skill. I hope you can see the sort of abc system I am driving at. I hope you see that steps link together, even as we change weight. We are producing new steps as we progress naturally, so that these new steps become small words. And, of course, then small sentences.

A tap exercise, or as we shall call it, an amalgamation is a kind of short sentence. Really good and musical exercises are sentences with real meaning.

So, let's keep up this method of learning – a new skill of any kind will require a vocabulary; it has to have one if it is to be learnt at all.

I have always believed that first you have to hear the sound in your head and then your feet *copy* that sound. In this book I want to give you examples of popular songs (or popular as far as that word goes!) so that you can tap the tune with your feet – *you will be using the abc footwork with the do re mi headwork!*

Major point:

We undoubtedly have to think about two things at once – the physical action in the feet and the rhythm or map they are to follow.

Going back to the *I Got Rhythm* step earlier, it is perhaps very useful to know the tune because the feet will then have that road map. To that end, let's repeat:

● **Relax** – sing the song in your head, over and over

● **Remind** – say, in your mind, the steps you are to use

● **Rewind** – go over the steps slowly, even out of context

● **Repeat** – practise it all again and again, getting it to feel right.

Provided you stick to the methodical approach, it will all make sense and it will all come together. And, of course, it should all sound musical, as with any instrument. At this stage in learning to tap dance, following a tuneful path is the most comfortable way to go. The rhythm is already decided so we just have to design the physical action. But here is the crucial and eye-opening point – once we can do this, and the possibilities are so numerous even here, we can then have the most incredible fun making up our own rhythm across the one on the soundtrack we are working with.

So, our own rhythm and our own design to illustrate it – now we are tap dancing! To a bare bones soundtrack – and we could get as bare boned as a metronome or a single drum beat – we are then able to express ourselves endlessly.

To get to the point where we have learnt enough steps to cope with many pieces of music is actually the tap dancer's stated aim. Rather like a blank canvas, we have in our mind a picture or a creative end point. We have the tools – our tap shoes – and we have the colours – our steps.

The shoes have the toe tips, toe taps, ball, heel and the flat. But they all can do more than one thing themselves: the toe tap can brush, beat, scuff, tap and the flat can be heavy or light, brushed, with weight or not. Quite a tool box! Quite a paint box!

All right then, let's have a few examples. I want to start with the song *Honeysuckle Rose* by Fats Waller, and we will only use the steps we have so far introduced. We will put together mini combinations and we will do it all in abbreviated vocabulary and with lyrics and diagram.

Honeysuckle Rose

Ev'ry honey bee, fills with jealousy, when they see you out with me. I don't blame them, goodness knows, honeysuckle rose.

Count it as below, using the circle method: this is the *rhythm only* of the words and as you can see, when I am describing the rhythm of the words, the diagram is on one side of the page; the rhythm for the steps is on the other side of the page.

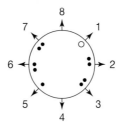

1 a2 a3 ___ 5 a6 a7 ___

Ev'ry honey bee, fills with jealousy,

figure 9.1

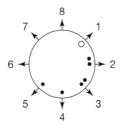

1 a2 a3 4 5 ___ ,

when they see you out with me.

figure 9.2

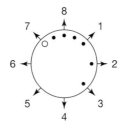

7 and 8 and 1 2 3 ___ ___ ___

I don't blame them, goodness knows,

figure 9.3

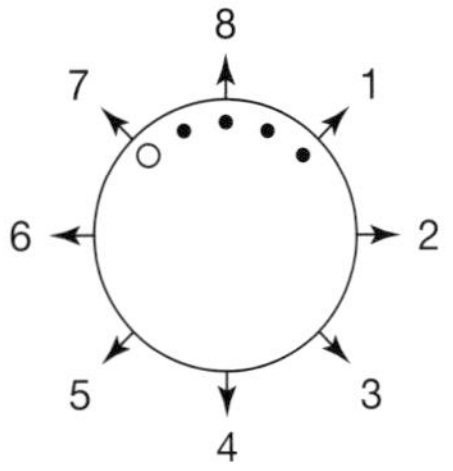

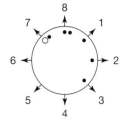

7 and 8 and 1 __ __ __ __ __
__ __.

honeysuckle rose.

figure 9.4

Major point:

Begin always on the ○.

- Read clockwise – and like a ticking clock, the tempo keeps on going, while you are pausing. (We cannot, for instance, count '123 __ __ __7' and come back in on '4' after pausing. The next number would be '7'. A clock or time or tempo does not stop.)

- Say only the ●.

Okay then, that is how to count the rhythm. Now, let's put our own tap rhythm on to that rhythm.

Put on track 13 of the CD.

Amalgamation to *Honeysuckle Rose*
Ev'ry honey bee,   fills with jealousy,

stp shfl bl-hl   stp shfl bl-hl

L   R   R   L   R   R

1   a2 a3 __   5   a6 a7 __

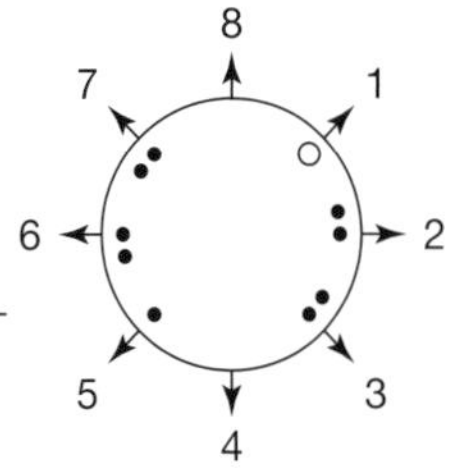

figure 9.5

when they see you out with me.

stp   shfl bl-ch stp   stp

L   R   R-L   R   L

1   a2   a3   4   5   __

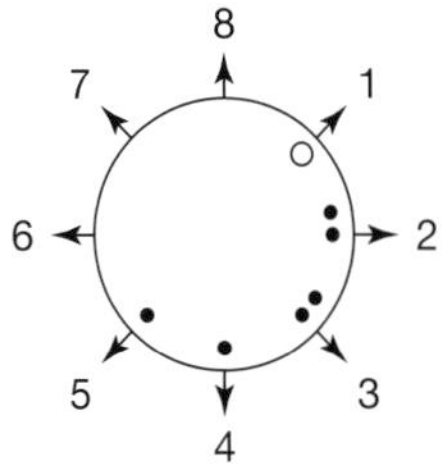

figure 9.6

I don't blame them, goodness knows,

bl-hl bl-hl stp stp stp

R   L   R   L   R

7a   8a   1   2   3   __ __ __

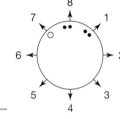

figure 9.7

honeysuckle rose.

spr   shfl bl-ch

L   R   R-L

7   a8   a1   __ __ __ __

__ __ __

figure 9.8

Do all of this on the right side. Then, because you have finished on the L foot, the R foot is free to begin again on the other side.

Right side, left side – remember the 'this is your left foot, this is your right' note, earlier in the book? Here we have the whole thing on the right side but of course, our very first sound is on the L foot.

Well, I think it is obvious the action takes place in the R, don't you? Even though the actual first step is in the L foot, we do all of the principal steps beginning on the R.

Just think that a juggler has to have both hands doing exactly the same thing, throwing, catching, etc. We have to get both sides to match completely. So, whatever we do on one side we have to mirror on the other.

Now, have a go – **Trap, Clap, Tap.**

Then, **Relax, Remind, Rewind, Repeat.**

We have used only those elements of our 'abc' above, nothing else. Provided you can hum this tune in your head, you can hopefully move your feet to it. Only tap on the words for now.

The next stage would be to embellish this basic idea with your own rhythm over the given rhythm. The possibilities are quite enormous, using our heads and our 'paint box' of sounds.

Now, let's try a different song. We will use the same elements but produce a different result. It's *Pick Yourself Up* by Jerome Kern.

Amalgamation to *Pick Yourself Up*
Put on track 14 of the CD.

Nothing's impossible I have found,

stp	stp	shfl	shfl	bl	hl	stp	
R	L	R	R	R	R	L	
1	2	a3	a4	5	6	7	__

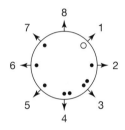

figure 9.9

for when my chin is on the ground ...

bl-ch		br br stp		br br stp				
R-L		R		L				
a1	2	3	4	5	6	7	__	

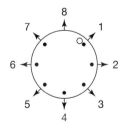

figure 9.10

I pick myself up, I dust myself off

shfl	bl-ch	stp		shfl	bl-ch	stp	
R	R-L	R,		L	L-R	L	
a1	a2	3	__	a5	a6	7	__

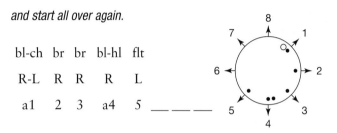

figure 9.11

and start all over again.

bl-ch	br	br	bl-hl	flt				
R-L	R	R	R	L				
a1	2	3	a4	5	__	__	__	__

figure 9.12

Repeat this one on the same side. The br br is a sort of slow shuffle.

When you are confident do the other side.

- **Relax** – it's a skill you are learning
- **Remind** – yourself of the tempo, melody (tune)
- **Rewind** – on the steps you are using your 'abc' vocabulary.
- **Repeat** – in your head, hands and feet. **Trap, Clap, Tap.**

And a nice third example to *Anything Goes* by Cole Porter.

Amalgamation to *Anything Goes*
Put on track 12 of the CD.

In olden days a glimpse of stocking was

bl-ch	stp	stp	br	br	shfl		bl-hl
R-L	R	L	R	R	R		R
a1	2	3	4	5	6and	___	a8

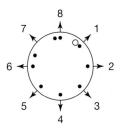

figure 9.13

looked on as some thing shocking but now God

bl-ch		bl-ch	bl-ch	bl-ch	stp	stp
			(Weaving)			
L-R		L-R	L-R	L-R	L	R
1and	___	a3	4and	___ a6	7	8

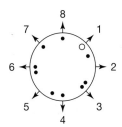

figure 9.14

knows ... anything

stp	___	___	___	___	___	shfl	stp
L to side (dragging R into L)				R			R
1	___	___	___	___	___	7and	8

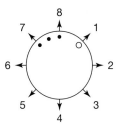

figure 9.15

goes ...

stamp	___	___	___	___	___	___	___
L		___	___	___	___	___	___
1		___	___	___	___	___	(8)

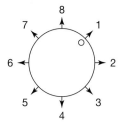

figure 9.16

To weave, go to the left with the L, and then cross over in front with the R, behind with the R, front with the R, behind with the R. See pictures 9.1a–d. At the end step L, then R to right side.

To drag, step L to left side and drag the R foot into L, but using all of the counts from 1 to 6. On '7 and 8', do shuffle step; on '1', do flat and hold this for 2 to 7.

'(8)' would actually be the next word in the song ('*Good* authors, too, who once knew better words, now only use four-letter words, writing prose, anything goes').

Relax......Remind......Rewind......Repeat....!

picture 9.1a   Weaving …

picture 9.1b

picture 9.1c

picture 9.1d

Major point:

Syncopation is sometimes a little difficult to grasp at first. As I stated earlier, it is all about stressing. We usually stress the numbers but we can also stress the spaces. These are the 'and' and the 'a'. This alternate stressing gives us our rhythm and it is a prerequisite of jazz music itself.

So, in the second bar above, the counting looks quite tricky. It obviously helps if you know the tune, and if you have the tune, play it and you can hear for yourself.

Keep going over it; use the counts and the spaces; look at the circles; sing the tune.

Trap the rhythm in your head; **Clap** in your hands; **Tap** the rhythm in your feet.

Now let's try the song *We Go Together* from the show *Grease*.

Amalgamation to *We Go Together*
Put on track 15 of the CD. See figure 9.17.

We go together like

	stp	stp	stp	stp		side stp	(drag)	stp
___	R	L	R	L		R		L
___	2	3	4	5	___	and	___	8

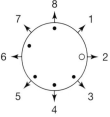

figure 9.17

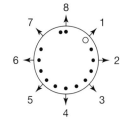

figure 9.18

See figure 9.18.

rama lama lama la keding a de dinga dong

shfl	bl-ch	shfl	bl-ch	shfl	bl-ch	bl-ch
R	R-L	R	R-L	R	R-L	R-L
1and	2and	3and	4and	5and	6and ___	a8

And now a theme tune, not a song, from the *Pink Panther* series.

Amalgamation to the *Pink Panther* theme
Put on track 16 of the CD. See figure 9.19.

tp-stp	tp-stp		tp-stp		tp-stp	shfl	bl-ch
R	L		R		L	R	R-L
a8	a1	___	a3	___	a5	a6	a7

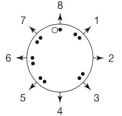

figure 9.19

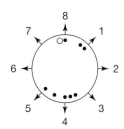

figure 9.20

See figure 9.20.

flp	bl-ch............	stp	stp	stp	stp	stp
R	L-R............	L	R	L	R	L(tgthr)
a8	a1 ... ___ ___	and	a	4	and 5	___ ___ .

Travel these last five steps to the R side and join the feet at the end.

Relax and then **Remind** yourself of the steps needed; then **Rewind** the sound and order of the steps; finally **Repeat** with the feet!

We are hopefully now in the happy position of hearing the tune in its basic rhythmic form and being able to copy that form with the foot sounds I have given you.

And now for some new letters – new steps for our tool box.

New steps

You can probably already see that putting a brush and a step together will give us a new step. This is more commonly known as a tap-step (tp-stp) and is also known as a flap (flp), especially in America.

A forward tap, which is the brush in question, and the landing of that onto the ball gives us this tap-step or flap. Because these are separate items anyway in this sub-section, I think it is best to describe each one. More 'letters' in our vocabulary.

Tap-step (tp-stp)

Begin with weight on L and raise the R behind, knee bent but not way back. Flex the foot, toe lifted and bring it forward with a brushing action using the toe tap only. Do this a few times and have the idea that you are brushing and flexing so that the feeling is one of pushing the tap forward and up. Now land the toe tap down in front to give the tap-step down to the floor with TWO sounds – a tiny brush (use a small action) and the second sound, a hard transfer of weight onto the ball and toe tap. So, it is a brush to ball action but short and down.

This is a closely coupled sound and has a feeling of being quite sharp and bright (pictures 9.2a–c).

Flap (flp)

Briefly described here, the flap is a very useful and great little step, not unlike the tap-step. However, and it is a big 'however', the action is completely different. But it does have the same sound – a1 a2 a3 a4. There is a big difference in the way the leg lifts and the way it lands. The knee is up in front (not swinging behind) as well as the foot. The ankle is flexed and ready to strike in a down and forward manner, and it lands on an almost locked knee! It is not unlike marching except the hips are allowed to throw out sideways as you step onto each foot (pictures 9.3a–c).

The flap can be a forward walking step, and get you off the spot, but it is better done in one place, on the spot.

So, the foot does not lift behind, but in front; the knee does not stay down but lifts, also in front; the leg does not bend on landing. If you can understand this step you will be on the way to mastering a very attractive and speedy move. And you can then practise it and not tire yourself because you will have found an 'economy of movement' that allows you to go faster and faster. You will love this step but it is tricky at first.

picture 9.2a   Tap-step …

picture 9.2b

picture 9.2c

picture 9.3a Flap …

picture 9.3b

picture 9.3c

Count it so: 'a1 a2 a3 a4 a5 a6 a7 a8', an accented sound and using alternate feet. Just a note: this is not the flap to be found in some syllabus' pages.

Spring (spr)

Begin in either L or R and spring on the ball to the other foot. This step achieves more speed on transfer and is not just a simple change of weight, but a more dynamic change of weight. It has a different energy and is meant to go right into the floor. An example would be:

stp	stp	spr	shfl	bl-ch			
R	L	R	L	L-R			
1	2	3	a4	a5	__	__	__

- '1' Step normally on the ball of foot.
- '2' Step normally.
- '3' Spring down, so aiding the shuffle 'a4' and also speeding up to our ball-change 'a5'. Remember to step on the ball of foot.

On this step really try to emphasize the spring down action because it *is* an emphatic thing.

Springing into a flat foot is called a drop (drp) and will be heavier.

Tap-spring (tp-spr)

I will use this step rarely because it gives the dancer a different upward feeling to the one I want, which is downward. To spring *up*, in my opinion, is to practise a different style, with a different feeling and I think it is, well, kind of old-fashioned! Oops!

We will need this to do our *time steps*, coming up, so I will describe it here.

Stand with weight on L, lift R foot up behind, brush the toe tap forward and spring onto the R, landing with heavier weight change on the ball of the R. Two sounds in place.

What tends to happen now is that the other leg lifts behind, which is what I do not want, but which will nevertheless occur. If you were to do this you achieve a rather immature looking action in the legs and body and I just don't want you looking that way in this style. It is too similar to a syllabus look, in my mind.

Hop (hp)

With the weight completely on one foot, either L or R, jump from that foot to itself – from one foot to the same foot. Remember, if you do the spring – from one foot to the other – it can look like a hop. But, a hop is as I have just described, with the crucial point being that it is not a weight change, of course!

In this style, do not hop up, but do hop down and with attitude! In other words, use a 'pressing' action or short sharp downward action. I think the hop should be as short as possible, with almost no air to be seen between foot and floor.

You know, gravity is the thing to defeat in dance. In ballet we try to defeat gravity by attempting to stay off the floor. But in tap dancing we like the floor; it's our friend; it's our drum! But we have to beat it into submission. In fact, it's the only dance in which I want you to *gain weight*! Only joking.

Joking, yes, but with the spring and the hop, I do want you to momentarily gain weight, in a flash. This will add to the dynamics of this style and give you that grounded sense, while at the same time keeping you light on your feet.

Stamp and stomp

I have referred above to a thing called a flat in one of the combinations. Now I can elaborate on this below.

Begin in either foot and lift the knee in front, ankle flexed. Bring the foot down and completely flat with one dynamic sound and either transfer weight (stamp) or do not transfer (stomp). We can use either, but although they do look and sound almost the same, they are two different things in that one changes weight and one does not. Let me put it this way, if you get these two mixed up you will be on the wrong foot and thus 50 per cent wrong! A big percentage.

Right, now do a full-bodied sound of a bass drum into the floor – enjoy this one.

10 basic rhythm combinations

In this chapter you will learn:

- more additions
- to connect with confidence
- to connect with tradition.

In this chapter, we will cover those kinds of steps and exercises that we need to go further with this dance skill. The *time step* has, and deserves to have, a chapter all to itself but it will be of some benefit to go through the set of moves required to achieve this bold new watershed.

I must stress that the time step is not a beginner's step and indeed it is already a misnomer – it is not a step at all, but an amalgam or series of steps or pieces (or letters and words, if we use our analogy so far). It obviously has the word 'step' attached to it because it is such an iconic thing in tap dance and there are many steps that are in the international lexicon that tap dancers would immediately recognize. We will come to these.

So, we need our 'abc', or our 'c-a-t / b-a-t' words idea. And for our purposes we will use the following:

- letters – brush, ball, hop, spring, step
- words – shuffle, shuffle hop, tap-spring, tap-step.

Using our previously learnt initial elements, we can order those elements into a small structure; our small words will make small sentences; our sentences will become longer; our paragraphs will make a musical sense and something called a tap routine will eventually follow.

We will need then: a shuffle, a hop, a spring, a tap-step, and a change of weight through a step (onto the ball).

But wait – what is a time step anyway?

Historically, every dancer on the old stages of America and Great Britain, had their own particular timing step. This would set them apart from other dancers and be identified with them whenever and wherever they went to perform. Each act – and, it must be said, most of these acts were male, or sometimes family acts that could include females – would invent a step or 'signature' to give to the band at each venue at which it appeared, and an understanding would be formed between band and artist at the beginning of his 'turn'.

In this way each could get the feel of how the rest of the turn would go on from there. Not everyone was good at their profession and this mutuality had to become standard practice all over the touring circuits to gain some kind of continuity and respect!

In the early days of American Minstrelsy and Vaudeville, from before the middle to the end of the nineteenth century, there would have been thousands of acts of all kinds and hundreds of theatres and halls to perform in. All of the great known and unknown tap-dancing acts of those times would have to go through this touring – and very tough – baptism in order to perfect their craft.

The dancers of those days had to be good at their craft because if they were not, they starved from lack of money earnt. Today, this sort of situation is unheard of. However, it was this very fact that was crucial to tap dancing evolving into the art form that it became. The constant practising, watching and listening (and stealing from each other) drove these dancers to often great lengths in a career that was, at best, very hard work in a tough and uncompromising life. Tap itself benefited because it eventually became the highly skilled dance that we sometimes see on film. The grind and sweat and improvization needed to perform and thus survive, would serve to drive tap up into the realms of professional dance, and not just a social pastime.

The Hollywood films that most of us know and love where tap dancing figured prominently, starred such great and wonderful dancers who appeared almost to dance on air on mirrored studio floors. I can assure you that at first it would have been old and smelly floorboards of theatres in some back-of-beyond part of the American countryside in among the heat and dust and the snow and ice!

Even the great Fred Astaire and his sister Adele – beginning their dancing careers at the age of 4 and 5 – had to go through this experience to hone their act together. It was years later that they would be the toast of Broadway and the darlings of London's West End, dancing for the King and the Prince of Wales.

Before they arrived in England in 1928, they had 'played every rat trap and chicken coop in America', according to Mr Astaire himself in his autobiography *Steps in Time*. That privation and determination is what made Fred Astaire the great dancer he was.

He was fortunate in that he was born into the sort of old American money that came over from old Europe in the late-nineteenth century. He was from Austria and his real name was Frederick Austerlitz. Fortunate also because he had a mother to whom apparently nobody would say no, and she proved to be the driving force in forging his illustrious career. She literally gave up her work to manage her children!

Other tap dancers, at one time originating from Africa, were not as fortunate, but were just as hungry for success – and probably more so. The competition between tap acts, endured during long months on the road, performing in the old towns and cities, and belonging to sometimes huge travelling caravan or tent type shows, ensured the success of tap itself. The dance became the most popular of all dances seen on stage and reigned supreme for years. In fact, for about 50 years in all.

In this time the Irish and the African dancers were the world's greatest and tap dancing was always belonging to these two camps equally. The Irish jig and reel dancers and the African tribal heritage collided and mixed to the sounds of the busy streets and boulevards of early bustling North American cities, and especially New York and Harlem. In the south it was in such places as Louisiana and New Orleans – the birthplace of jazz itself. In the country parts of America, tap was also created but from ancient African tribal traditions of movement and rhythm.

Great musicians and entertainers were born around these times. People such as Eubie Blake, Scott Joplin, Louis Armstrong and Fats Waller were all to become world famous. But the dancers were not so well known. Dancers such as George Primrose, Willie Covan, Eddie Rector and Bert Williams were the forerunners of dancers such as Bill 'Bojangles' Robinson, John Bubbles and Fred Astaire.

There were some great brother acts too. The Nicholas Brothers, The Berry Brothers and many more. Also, there were female soloists such as Dorothy Wing, Jeni Le Gon and Peggy Ryan.

Further reading will give you more of such information and I am happy to point you in the direction of some titles in Taking it further at the end of this book.

It was always said that the Irishman/European brought the body and the footwork skills and the African brought the rhythm. I would agree with this and it seems to me a perfect meeting of minds and cultures. Up until the time of this turbulent mixing, western dance was only in 3/4 time. The African brought the propulsive rhythm and the timing soon to become known as 4/4 – an even and equal number of counts in the bar and easy enough for anyone to understand. A 'popular' music and the beginning of 'pop' music itself.

Jazz was built on the 4/4 time and thus was tap dancing also. The story of jazz music is the same story as that of tap dance. But, the dancer came before the music! The counts in 4 and in 8 were invented around this, at the turn of the century, and the jazz age was under way.

So to the story of the time step, an everlasting and evolving dance count that suited everyone. A new language, then in its infancy, used to great effect between dancer and musician. A new way of understanding where each other was coming from and a way of moving tap forward for the future generations. These early time steps are alive and well today, and just as new to the dancer coming across them for the first time. To him or her they are new. They are of course changed, but the principles are the same.

Today they are among the standard figures of tap dance. Other figures have survived too. Have you heard of these: Maxie-Ford, Susie Q, Buffalo Break and Falling off a Log? No? Well, you have now! All are known figures (to tap dancers) and all are still in use.

The basic figure time steps and their many elaborations give the tap dancer a touchstone wherever he or she is in the world. You could go to a tap class in Sydney and to a tap class in Toronto and to one in Liverpool, and you would do the same thing, or near equivalent. An international set of steps and ingredients.

It is hard or even impossible to know for certain who invented the steps we use as standard today, but Marshall and Jean Stearns' book, *Jazz Dance. The Story of American Vernacular Dance* tells us they were invented by a man called King Rastus Brown.

But, there is one time step that has actually remained the same and because of tradition and respect has always been regarded as somehow sacrosanct. In Chapter 11 we will learn the *Shim Sham* and its derivations and history. This is the 'hoofer's' own time step, born long ago and loved still today. A time step in its pure form, still in its original rhythm.

First, though, we are going to look at the single, double and triple time steps.

They can all be added to, however, and can become quite complex in execution once you have mastered these basic three. For instance, one simple time step could be become a 'single, double-pick-up time step'; a 'double, double-pick-up time step'; or a 'triple-pick-up wing time step' and so on, using the add-on system that I have used so far.

We will deal here only with the single, double and triple basics and first I will explain why they are called these names and give you another meaning as well, but which is not often realized. A very clever step.

In each case, we will begin on count 8. This is because the heavy next step (the hop) will be strongly felt on the first downbeat of 1. Going on to the next count of 2 is where the single or the double or the triple label is placed.

Listen to tracks 38, 39 and 40 of the CD. You will hear:

- One (single) sound on count '2' in the first time step …

- Two (double) sounds on the count of '2' in the next time step …

- Three (triple) sounds on the count of '2' in the next time step …

Using our counting knowledge gained so far, these counts will be:

- Single '8 and 1 (2)' . . . a quarter measure '1......2'

- Double '8 and 1 (and 2)' . . . an eighth measure '1 and 2'

- Triple '8 and 1 (and a 2)' . . . a twelfth measure '1 and a 2'

Look back at Chapter 08 Rhythm and counting explained and see this note value section. It is hopefully not too difficult to grasp that we do need to know and understand rhythm. By dividing notes into half or quarter or more, we accommodate more sounds; by stressing these notes in alternate and inventive ways, we can produce clever rhythms.

Having one, two or three sounds in this one place gives us the labels of single, double or triple. But, and here is news, the single time step uses a quarter note; the double time step uses an eighth note; and the triple uses a twelfth note.

These are labels not usually given to time steps but that is in fact what they are – expressing three note values we use in tap all of the time.

It follows that if we used four sounds and thus produce a quadruple time step, we are then using a sixteenth note time step, which would look like this:

- Quad '8 and 1 (and and a 2)'; a sixteenth measure '1 and and a 2'

Coming up now are some exercises and combinations leading to the time step because, as mentioned, it is not a beginner's step but a series of moves that add up to a beautifully rounded figure. It will eventually give you enormous pride upon achievement.

Remember:

You must completely change weight when stepping; you must do exactly what the step says; you have to keep up with the time you set your counts to – 8 1 2 3 4 5 6 7.

Exercise 1

shfl	hp	shfl	hp	shfl	hp	shfl	hp
R	L	R	L	R	L	R	L

8 and 1 2 and 3 4 and 5 6 and 7

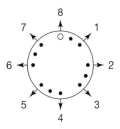

figure 10.1

Exercise 2

tp-stp tp-stp tp-stp tp-stp tp-stp tp-stp tp-stp tp-stp

L	L	L	L	L	L	L	L
a1	a2	a3	a4	a5	a6	a7	a8

Keep this on one foot for now and get the feeling of *momentarily* transferring weight each time.

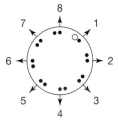

figure 10.2

Exercise 3

tp-stp stp; tp-stp stp; tp-stp stp; tp-stp stp

L R; L R; L R; L R

a1 <u>and</u> a2 <u>and</u> a3 <u>and</u> a4 <u>and</u>

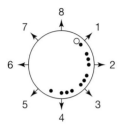

figure 10.3

Exercise 4

stp shfl stp shfl stp shfl stp shfl stp shfl stp

R L L R R L L R R L L

1 and 2 and 3 and 4 and 5 and 6 and 7 and 8 and

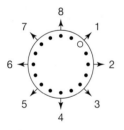

figure 10.4

Practise this step in two ways:

- Firstly, one triplet at a time, i.e. on the same foot – shfl-stp, shfl-stp, shfl-stp, shfl-stp. When you are comfortable, link the steps L and R so that it becomes continuous and do one shuffle-step on each side in turn.

- Secondly, now linking the steps, be sure to do this even sound across the work, using our eighth notes rhythm. Start on the step and link them in this other way – and 1 and 2 and 3 and 4.

Exercise 5

spr tp-stp stp spr tp-stp stp

R L R L R L

___ 2 and 3 and ___ ___ 6 and 7 and ___

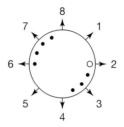

figure 10.5

This last, please do the combination on '2 and 3 and' because that is exactly where it occurs in the time step on the right side.

You can simply count yourself in '5, 6, 7, 8' and also '1', before moving on '2'! Remember that although you will not sound '1' you are still using it in your clock way of timing. Missing it out only means not sounding it; we are still using it.

On the L side it will occur on '6 and 7 and' because that is the mirrored side of our 8 counts, if you see.

The time step on the R side will take four counts, 8 1 2 3, and on the L side will take the other four counts, 4 5 6 7.

But – and here is the very important counting – it will read thus:

8 and <u>1</u>, <u>2</u> and 3 <u>and</u>, 4 and <u>5</u>, <u>6</u> and 7 <u>and</u>

Try to really stress by landing hard those underlined counts. This will accentuate the rhythm.

Okay, here we go!

Single time step

1. Stand in the L, R raised in front with knee lifted and foot ready to

2. shuffle on '8 and'. Then hop on the L on '1'.

3. Put the R down slightly behind, on the ball only. Transfer the weight as you spring onto this foot on '2'. Changing weight completely here is nothing short of essential, because you will have freed the L to do a tap-step in a forward action on 'and 3'.

4. Next transfer weight into the last step on the ball of the R foot. To do that you must have transferred weight into the L in the tap-step. Count this last one 'and'. This timing is clearly heard on track 38 of the CD.

Stand	L
Shuffle	R
Hop	L in place
Spring	R behind
Tap-step	L forward
Step	R beside L

Single time step – the 'single' refers to the spring onto the R – 1 sound.

Count it so:

shfl	hp	spr	tp-stp	stp		shfl	hp	spr	tp-stp	stp
R	L	R	L	R		L	R	L	R	L
8 and	1	2	and 3	and;		4 and	5	6	and 7	and

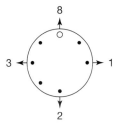

figure 10.6 right side

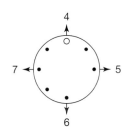

figure 10.7 left side

Each side takes four counts. If a time step repeats in the style written about in this book – an American or jazz style – it will use 8s and not 4 counts for each side. The counting of dance in 8s is a distinctly American invention, and gives the body more time to handle the standard 4 counts in a bar, as counted by most musicians. In this way a dancer's bar is two 4s, or one 8.

In Chapter 11 The Shim Sham, this famous American time step uses this counting in 8s. The Shim Sham came along in the jazz era and it is easy to hear this type of early jazz music in counts of 8, as well as 4. If you listen it is possible to count it both ways because of its construction.

In the introduction I mentioned that there are as many styles in tap dance as there are in jazz dance. A piano player, after learning the skill, will adopt a style and it is simply inevitable. The same tool-box, the same colours – piano, fingers and keys – but everyone has their own touch or style.

Tap is like ballet but only in respect of the fact it is a dance language, and that it has a set of basic moves with certain characteristics. Steps such as shuffles and pick-ups are similar to say, plies and tondus. These can then be interpreted and re-interpreted as the style denotes. To *teach* tap like ballet, however, I think is a mistake unless it is under constant pressure to improvize.

The European way of counting a time step of four counts in each side and the American way of eight counts in each side, leads to great differences in technique and invention.

But don't worry – we will come to those longer time steps later!

> **Remember:**
>
> A time step does *four* things:
>
> **1.** Wherever it begins it will end on the next previous number. So, begin on '8', end on '7'; begin on '3', end on '2'; begin on '1', end on '8'. But they *usually* begin on '8' or '4', which are the off beats.
>
> **2.** It repeats exactly the same over both sides.
>
> **3.** Traditionally in the American way, it uses 3 × 8s for the time step and 1 × 8 for the break (or of course, using the other time step, 3 × 4 and 1 × 4).
>
> **4.** It keeps you in time!

The single, double, triple is a basic set of figures used over many years and is a traditional and beautifully round figure.

Can I refer you now to Chapter 08 on Rhythm and counting explained? The note values are: whole note; half note; quarter note; eighth note; twelfth note; sixteenth note – 1 1/2 1/4 (usually the tempo measure) 1/8th 1/12th 1/16th.

And the other one I mentioned – the accented eighth note – 1/8th acc.

The clever time step uses the quarter, the eighth and the twelfth like so:

- Single – between the '1' and the '2', we see nothing … just '1..2', a 1/4 note.

- Double – between the '1' and the '2', we see 'and' … '1 and 2' … , an 1/8th note.

- Triple – between the '1' and the '2', we see 'and a'… '1 and a 2'… a 1/12th note.

So, we call these time steps something else – a quarter note time step; an eighth note time step; a twelfth note time step. Listen to tracks 38 to 41 of the CD and hear this addition of the extra counts.

Double time step

1. As before, begin with weight on L, with R in front, ready to shuffle on '8 and'. Shuffle the R and hop on the L on '1'.

2. Now, tap-spring forward onto the R, landing slightly behind the L on 'and2', releasing the L immediately by fully transferring weight. The L now does a tap-step in a forward action on 'and3'. The R now closes up to it by landing on the ball on 'and', again completely changing weight. The tap-spring lands heavier.

Use CD track 39.

Stand	L	
Shuffle	R	
Hop	L in place	Double time step – the 'double' refers to the tap-spring onto the R – 2 sounds.
Tap-spring	R forward	
Tap-step	L forward	
Step	R beside L	

Count it so:

shfl	hp	tp-spr	tp-stp	stp;	shfl	hp	tp-spr	tp-stp	stp.
R	L	R	L	R;	L	R	L	R	L
8and	1	and 2	and 3	and;	4and	5	and 6	and 7	and

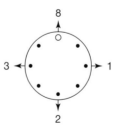

figure 10.8 right side.
Four counts to a bar

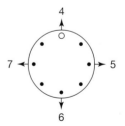

figure 10.9 left side.
Four counts to a bar

Triple time step

1. As before, begin with weight on the L with R in front ready to shuffle on '8 and'. Shuffle on the R and hop on the L on '1'.

2. Now, shuffle-step onto the R, but to the R side and landing feet together on 'and a 2'. You must transfer the weight every time you see 'step' and thus here too. You have now released the L, and do as before with the tap-step forward action on 'and 3'. The R closes up to it by landing on the ball on 'and'. Completely change weight.

Use CD track 40.

Stand	L	
Shuffle	R in front	
Hop	L in place	Triple time step – the 'triple' refers to the shuffle step on the R – 3 sounds.
Shuffle-step	R from the side, land together	
Tap-step	L forward	
Step	R beside L	

Count it so:

shfl hp shfl-stp tp-stp stp; shfl hp shfl-stp tp-stp stp

R   L   R   L   R;   L   R   L   R   L

8and 1 and a 2 and 3 and; 4 and 5 and a 6 and 7 and

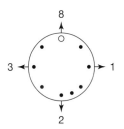

figure 10.10 right side. Four counts to a bar

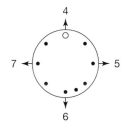

figure 10.11 left side. Four counts to a bar

Quadruple time step

The quadruple time step would read as follows:

1. As with the others, begin with weight on the L, R in front, ready to shuffle on '8and' and hop on the L on '1'.

2. Now, do a shuffle step-heel with the R, to the R side and place it, landing feet together on 'and and a 2'. Don't worry, I know it looks complicated but try it – it is only one extra sound. It is worth the effort to hear it done. You must again transfer weight every time you step. You have released the L at this point so now finish as before with a tap-step forward action on 'and3'.

3. The R closes up to it by landing on the ball on 'and', completely changing weight as always.

Use CD track 41.

Stand	L	
Shuffle	R in front	
Hop	L in place	Quadruple time step – the 'quadruple' refers to shuffle step-heel on the R – 4 sounds
Shuffle step-heel	R from the side, land together	
Tap-step	L forward	
Step	R beside L	

Count it so:

shfl hp shfl stp-hl tp-stp stp;   shfl hp shfl stp-hl tp-stp stp

R   L   R   L   R;   L   R   L   R   L

8and 1 and and a 2 and 3 and; 4and 5 and and a 6 and 7 and

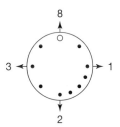

figure 10.12 right side. Four counts to a bar

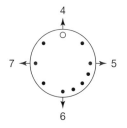

figure 10.13 left side. Four counts to a bar

The break

This is the end piece, the cap, the aim, the flourish – and of course it can be as individual as you are, once you get the idea. Here, though, we must stick to the standard break, because it is part of the whole standard.

Exercise 4 above will prepare you for this break. Also, if you look back to the page containing shuffle-step (page 47), you will see it counted as: 'and a 1, and a 2, and a 3, and a 4', and so on.

But, here we need to count it differently, while at the same time doing the same thing; we need to count it evenly or more smooth and flat in sound.

In these standard time steps the 'round' flows very well. We have the sides R and L, each of 4 counts; we then have the next 3 counts of the bar to begin a third side, but need to develop this into our break.

It is important then, to know when the break occurs and it does so after we have completed two sides and begun the third.

The break always begins in the *same* place, in the *same* foot and on the *same* count in all of these figures. That is to say it always begins on '2'. On the single '2', double 'and 2', and on the triple 'and a 2', and quadruple 'and and a 2'. Each has to land on this count, so from this count the break also occurs. Tracks 42 to 45 of the CD shows the break with the single, double, triple and quadruple and you can hear the even count from the '2'.

1. Do the three sides described above, using the single for now but you will end on the second count of '2'. The single time step:

8 and 1,	2 and 3 and	Right side
4 and 5,	6 and 7 and	Left side
8 and 1,	2 ...	Right side

2. From this spring on the count of '2', go into a shuffle-step on the L, then the R and then the L again, joining them together and making a continuous run of beats. Finish with a step on the R foot. Do these in an even rhythm.

Count it so:

2 and 3 and 4 and 5 6 and 7 (the next '8' will be the next time step, beginning on the other side. A perfect round, remember?)

And in rhythm:

spr	shfl	stp	shfl	stp	shfl	stp	stp
R	L	L	R	R	L	L	R
2	and 3	and	4 and	5	and 6	and	7

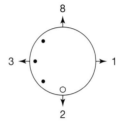
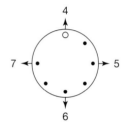

figure 10.14 right side. Four counts to a bar

figure 10.15 left side. Four counts to a bar

Let me remind you, we are using 8s because it's a dancer's way of counting! 2 × 4s are 8 and we are using here 2 × 8s or 4 × 4s in this standard time step.

Try to **Trap, Clap, Tap** here – it really helps.

Of course, by changing from single to double or triple or quad, when we add the one extra beat each time, we will affect the *whole* time step. The extra sounds on '2' give the break an added flavour and more sparkle.

Now, counting the whole thing in, say, triple time steps and break, look at the following and listen to the demonstration on track 46 of the CD. See figures 10.16–10.19.

shfl hp shfl-stp tp-stp stp; shfl hp shfl-stp tp-stp stp

8 and 1 (and a 2) and 3 and; 4and 5 (and a 6) and 7 and

shfl   hp   shfl-stp   shfl   stp   shfl stp shfl   stp   stp

8 and   1   (and a 2)   and 3   and   4 and   5   and 6   and   7.

I......................Break......................I

Good luck as you practise this! It is a great leap forward, using many of the elemental things we have learnt so far (see figures 10.16–10.19).

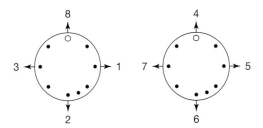

figure 10.16   **figure 10.17**

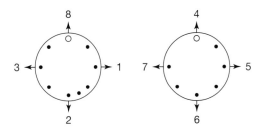

figure 10.18   **figure 10.19**

Now try this basic rhythm combination using time steps.

stp	stp	shfl	bl-ch	bl-hl	bl-hl	stp
L	R	L	L-R	L	R	L
1	2	a3	a4	5and ___	a7	8

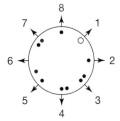

figure 10.20

1. Repeat on the right side, but only to '7'.

2. Then: do two single time steps, with break, using our usual '8and' (shfl) to begin (see figures 10.21–10.24).

shfl   hp   spr   tp-stp   stp;   shfl   hp   spr   tp-stp   stp

shfl   hp   spr   shfl   stp   shfl   stp   shfl   stp   stp

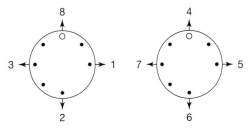

figure 10.21 right side   **figure 10.22** left side

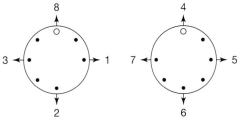

figure 10.23 right side   **figure 10.24** left side

3. Follow this with:

(going to the right side>>>)

bl-ch   bl-ch   shfl   bl-ch   bl-ch   shfhl   bl-ch   bl-ch

L-R   L-R   L   L-R   L-R   L   L-R   L-R

and 8 and 1 and 2 and 3 and 4 and 5 and 6 and 7

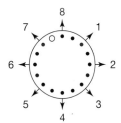

figure 10.25

4. Then:

(going to the left side >>>weaving<<<)

clap	stp	stp	stp	stp	stp	stp		spr
hands	L	R	L	R	L	R		L
8	1	2	3	4	5	6	__	and

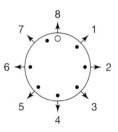

figure 10.26

(step side L, behind R, side L, front R, etc.)

Here, the 'and' after the missed '7' will be quite immediate, because it is a spring down.

5. Then:

shfl	hp	tp-spr	shfl-stp		shfl-stp		shfl-stp		stp
R	L	R	L		R		L		R
8 and	1	and 2	and 3	and	4	and 5	and	6 and	7

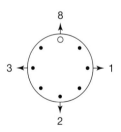 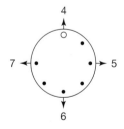

figure 10.27 right side   **figure 10.28** left side

6. Then:

stp	bl-ch	stp		stp	stp
L	R-L	R		L	R
__	1	__	a3	4	__	6	7

(bring feet firmly together on '7').

For the music this time use nothing at all – just the rhythm of the step itself. But if you can think of something in your collection that sounds like this one, then use it and dance to it. Now, you will really be connecting with your own sound in your own head.

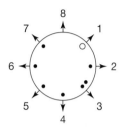

figure 10.29

Let's try another but this time to the tune of Gershwin's *Fascinatin' Rhythm*.

Remember:

We are now doing the two things we set out to do.

1. Sing or hum the tune and therefore the rhythm melody.

2. Put over the top of this, our own rhythm melody.

If you can do this you are now tap dancing, although you will only be using those basic steps and notes so far discussed in this book. Tap dancing well with few steps is actually very clever because you have to be more inventive and clear with minimum ingredients.

I will give you both here – the rhythm of the tune only, and then I will describe the rhythm of the routine to put over it. Using the diagram circles method, I hope you are now developing speed as well as knowledge (see figures 10.30–10.33).

Fascinatin' Rhythm

1 and 2 and 3 and __ a 5 and 6 and 7 __

1 and 2 and 3 and __ a 5 and 6 and __ __

1 and 2 and 3 and __ a 5 and 6 and 7 __

1 and 2 and 3 and __ a 5 and 6 and __ __

These will repeat again exactly.

You cannot fail to have noticed that these alternate lines are deliberately identical. This is a typical device of Gershwin's to give the impression (successfully) that the 'fascinating rhythm' he is talking about is incessant and repetitive. The song goes on to hear him plead for the rhythm to leave him alone because it is driving him crazy! But, back to the plot ...

This is a very clever and in fact quite complex song structure but I don't think it is too much for our purposes here.

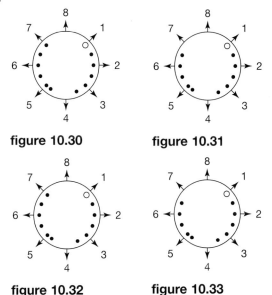

figure 10.30   **figure 10.31**

figure 10.32   **figure 10.33**

The words are as follows:

> Fascinatin' rhythm, you've got me on the go
> Fascinatin' rhythm, I'm all a quiver ...
> What a mess you're making! The neighbours want to know
> Why I'm always shaking just like a flivver ...

(Whatever a 'flivver' is! Actually it is a veteran American 'bone-shaker' car from about the 1920s.) But as a rhyme it does the job. George's brother Ira Gershwin was a prolific lyricist and his words to many songs will live in history, probably for ever.

Now for the feet routine:

stp shfl bl-ch stp; shfl bl-ch stp bl-ch

1. Do this on the R side, dropping onto R on count '1', and then on the L side, using the rhythms below (see figures 10.34 and 10.35).

2. Then do: double shuffle (shfl shfl), '1 and 2and' on the R; ball-change R-L; A three-beat paddle on R, L, R (see figure 10.36). Finally, do a stamp, stamp on L and R, followed by pick-up step on L and R and shuffle step-heel L, ball-heel R (see figure 10.37).

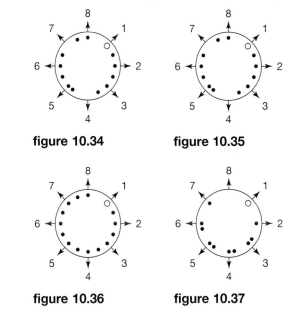

figure 10.34   **figure 10.35**

figure 10.36   **figure 10.37**

A quick final reminder about time steps, both European and American. The European is over 4 counts per side, the American over 8 counts per side. If you can add 4 counts of something to the European one, you will have 8 counts on each side. So for example, before doing the shfl hp of the single time step, just do, say, shfl stp stp, shfl stp stp on 8 and 1 and 2 and 3and, *then* go into the single.

Try it out with as many steps over 4 counts that you can think of.

11 the Shim Sham

In this chapter you will learn:

- about a wonderful set of steps steeped in history
- about a connection to the past that keeps tap up to date
- more about building a routine.

Track list

47	Shim Sham 1 sound
48	Shim Sham 2 sound
49	Shim Sham 3 sound
50	Shim Sham 4 sound
51	Hartley Shim Sham 4 sound

We come now to *the* most famous time step in history, the Shim Sham – or the Shim Sham Shimmy, as it's called among the well-informed!

This is a time step usually credited to one man and is not, as are those described above, the result of evolution from one person or era to another. His name was Leonard Reed and he was an ethnic American. He was typical of the kind of pioneering spirit that American artists of the time possessed, as a means of surviving as struggling dancers.

It has not altered since the 1920s, when Mr Reed invented it, and has now become a valued part of the lexicon of real tap dancing. Variations are allowed, and I am going to give you *my* version here in this book.

This time step is based on an 8 count round, using 8 counts per side, and 4 × 8s for the whole time step and break. So, R–8 counts; L–8 counts; on the R again–8 counts; R–break 8 counts.

The history of the Shim Sham is the history of tap dance in small form. In the early part of the twentieth century, dancing was immensely popular on the performing stage and there were thousands of dance acts; today, by comparison, there are virtually none at all. Any new thing, such as this step, was seized upon and used to perpetuate the whole idea of dancing for a living. In today's Hip Hop culture, exactly the same thing happens when steps are seen and used. Some aspects of dance do not change.

At the time of writing there are not many people who dance in an act for a living. Dancing was, and still is, the poor relation of the Arts. To be a singer – well, that's okay; to be an actor – yes, fine; but a dancer? It is often a case of, 'Well, if you really must ...'. In those early days dance acts proliferated and were very competitive.

The Shim Sham is a step invented for the music of its time and uses the straight 4/4, with such a simple construction that it is irresistible. It was sufficient to cover almost all of the current music and everyone adopted it. All tap acts added it to their set and it eventually became a beloved thing to perform. In America the Shim Sham is sacrosanct, but that does not mean it is old or old fashioned. Rather, it is respected for its contribution and for its musical simplicity. This is a time step written how it should be, using the 4 × 8 rounds, so giving the dancer more time with the step (oops, excuse the pun)! It is absolutely ideal for the usual 4/4 jazz phrasing and fits so many of the classic jazz pieces.

Downbeats (sometimes called on beats) are usually on the numbers 1, 3, 5, 7 and the upbeats (sometimes called off beats) on the numbers 2, 4, 6, 8 when we are counting tempo in quarter notes. However, when we use *double time*, i.e. counting 'and 1 and 2 and 3 and 4', etc, the 'and' becomes this upbeat and all the numbers are the downbeats. If we step on this 'and' and highlight it, or accent it we are stressing the beat that is not normally stressed and it all makes for a great syncopatory experience!

The first of four Shim Shams can be done with a shuffle, a paddle or a flat/pick-up.

Shim Sham 1

Use CD track 47.

1. Stand in the L, R ready to shuffle to the side diagonal. (When we use the paddle or the flat/pick-up, we will use them to the front.)

2. On the count '8 and 1', do a shuffle-step on the R foot.

3. On the count '2 and 3', do a shuffle-step on the L foot.

4. On the next R, do a shuffle ball-change, immediately followed by another shuffle-step. Try it now, but do all landings on the ball! Go through the centre spot on all changes.

Count it so:

shfl-stp	shfl-stp	shfl	bl-ch	shfl-stp
R	L	R	R-L	R
8 and 1	2 and 3	4 and	5 and	6 and 7

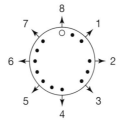

figure 11.1 right side

Do the 'shuffle ball-change, shuffle-step' quite crisply achieving a snappy seven sounds on the R side: '4 and 5 and 6 and 7'!

5. Repeat all of this on the L side.

6. Then, on the R side again, do everything as before but *rest* the very last sound (the R ball of foot) next to the L. You will need to use it again straight away.

7. You have done three sides and now you will do the break to complete the whole Shim Sham 1.

The break

A very cute break coming up, following the set-up from the time step.

1. You are now in the position of having the R resting beside the L, with no weight in the foot.

2. Using this R foot, step to the side, landing on the ball of foot, with heel lifted and on count '8'. Put the heel down on '1' (8 1).

3. Bring the *tip of the toe* of the L behind the R foot, neatly tucked in, and land it on '2' (8 1 2). You can see this foot in a mirror (see picture 11.1a) to the right of the R foot. Balance must be 100 per cent in the R at this point: any heavier use of the L will mean you could transfer weight, even slightly, and it must not happen here.

4. Having the weight firmly in the R, you can hop on it and then step onto the L, on the ball to the left (see picture 11.1b). You are now in the L foot. Do the same hop action again and this time on that L foot. Now put the R down to complete the hop-step. You are now in the R, which is in place behind the L.

picture 11.1a   Toe tip behind R

picture 11.1b   Weight on ball

5. You are in a crossed position, R behind L momentarily (picture 11.1c) having done the count '3 and and 5' (no '4' because of syncopation). All that remains is to step *to the left* on the ball of each foot, L and R, finishing together. Rest the R beside L (pictures 11.1d and e).

picture 11.1c   Changing weight into R

picture 11.1d   Changing weight into L

picture 11.1e   Closing R to L and rest R

Count it so:

bl	hl	to	hp-stp	hp-stp	stp	stp
R	R	L	R-L	L-R	L	R(rest)
8	1	2	3 and ___	and 5	6	7

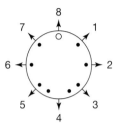

figure 11.2

Okay, now you're in the Tap Dancers' Club, we'll go on!

Shim Sham 1 (using paddles and flat/pick-up)

1. Stand on L, R ready to paddle in front. Beginning on the '8 and 1' do everything exactly the same, i.e. three sides, rhythm, ending with R foot resting, and get as far as the break. This can be slightly different also.

   For the Shim Sham 1 flat/pick-up: do everything as previously but use a flat/pick-up where the paddle just was. It is the same three sounds, but with a dynamic on the first one, and this could be used when the music you are dancing to suggests that heavier first beat. As you get better at this, you will see – and hear – this obvious point.

The break (for paddles and flat/pick-up)

2. Again to the R side, do the ball heel toe as before on 8 1 2.

3. Then: do heel-step, heel-step to replace the hop-step last time.

   On the second heel-step, find yourself in the middle, feet together.

4. Add this move instead of the previous L and R move:

   Drop onto both feet at once and apart then pull together on '7'. This will look and sound very slick! Well, it should anyway (picures 11.2a and b)!

picture 11.2a Drop apart

You have to try to find the timing for both feet and shoulders and it's almost impossible to explain. So, do one exercise first – the Shimmy – then do the feet next, separately. Then try to do them both at the same time. Good luck here! Seriously, though, it is the 'bees knees' when you have it. You are excused the Shimmy on the break!

picture 11.2b   Pull together

picture 11.3   The Shimmy, looking good!

The Shimmy

Now for the icing on the cake! Can you Shimmy? Can you rapidly move those shoulders alternately forward and backward in turn? This is a shoulder move but you will find other bits moving too! What the heck, enjoy it! BUT …

The trick is to do this Shimmy at the same time as doing the Shim Sham steps. It is quite a trick to master, so do it like this:

Look in your mirror and SHIMMY! … no, not too fiercely!

This is a true tap dancer's set – the Shim Sham Shimmy – done today as it always was, using swing and style and a bit of cheek to boot! This will now give you for perhaps the first time a routine that looks and sounds like a routine, not just making use of the feet, as we have done so far.

> **Note:**
>
> Track 47 on the CD gives you the whole Shim Sham with sides repeating one after the other, i.e. Shim Sham 1 on the R is followed by Shim Sham 1 on the L. Then it moves on to the same format with the others.

Shim Sham 2

This will connect instantly with Shim Sham 1, so you will find that to use the R foot immediately, you will *not* have the weight in the R, which you have just landed on the count '7'. If you use the paddle or the flat/pick-up version, your feet are closed at this point. Whichever you choose to do you must move your R foot first on Shim Sham 2. I will assume you have done the first Shim Sham.

Use CD track 48.

1. On the R, stamp to diagonal right front on '8' and put down the L on the ball on '1' in its own place, so that you are doing two sounds. Practise this move a few times using '8 1; 2 3; 4 5; 6 7' and so on. You will be doing flat on the R and ball on the L, and using a swinging action in the hips (you can also Shimmy if you like!). Go on, try it!

2. All right, do this twice – stamp ball; stamp ball; on the R L R L and on '8 1 2 3'.

3. Then: step down firmly on the ball of the R, keeping the heel lifted and on count '4'. Put the heel down hard '5', and bring the L over the R to land on the ball on 'and'. You are now in a crossover position (pictures 11.4a and c).

4. Quickly put the L heel down on 'and' and follow it immediately with the ball on the R on count '7', to right diagonal back (picture 11.4b). The picture from the back also included here may help to explain it (picture 11.4d).

5. The counting is cute but you need to hear it on the CD (track 48). Do it now.

picture 11.4a   Crossover

picture 11.4b   Heel-ball

picture 11.4c   *Crossover rear view*

picture 11.4d   *Heel-ball rear view*

Count it so:

stamp	bl	stamp	bl	stp	hl-bl	hl-bl
R	L	R	L	R	R-L	L-R
8	1	2	3	4	5and	__ and 7

.........three sides R.. L.. R

This will have the effect of travelling to the R and then L and to the R again, crossing over itself three times in all.

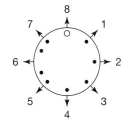

figure 11.3 right side

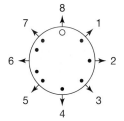

figure 11.4 left side

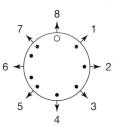

figure 11.5 right side

The break

The break is different here. Using the 'crossover rhythm' which is:

'4 5and and 7', and after completing the third side, you are now in the R foot to diagonal back at the end of this third side.

Cross back over the L foot with this rhythm!

Do it like this:

1. Do the third side, which is a copy of the first side, to stop in the right diagonal back position, shown in picture 11.4d. With the L, go into the ball on '8', beat the heel of that foot on '1', crossover with the R landing the ball on '<u>and</u>', beat the heel of that foot on 'and', put the ball of the L down to left diagonal back on '3'. You now have: '8 1 and __ and 3'.

2. Now, *repeat exactly on the other side* – with the R, go into the ball on '4', beat the heel of that foot on '5', crossover with the L, landing the ball on '<u>and</u>', beat the heel of that foot on 'and', put the ball of the R down to side on '7'. Note the underline on the ball and particularly stress this.

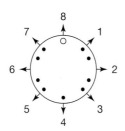

figure 11.6

stp	hl-bl	hl-bl	stp	hl-bl	hl-bl
L	L-R	R-L	R	R-L	L-R
8	1 and ___	and 3	4	5 and ___	and 7

Phew! I hope you got that!

I strongly suggest you now go to CD track 48 and hear it for yourself because I know you will like this snappy little time step.

Shim Sham 3 (the Tack Annie)

Use CD track 49.

This one is probably the hardest to learn, but it's also the one that breaks the rules! Oh gosh, I hope I cope, I hear you say! Worry not, yon virgin tapper, all is in hand – or in foot, of course. But what is it, this rule break? Well, it does all three sides – on the same side.

Oh yes, it also has the best name – and it really is called the Tack Annie. It is the hardest because it involves the pick-up; I know I have explained it a little already earlier in the book, but let's go over it again.

A pick-up (p-up) is the action of picking up the toe in a backward motion, up and off the floor. If you think of 'hingeing' the foot from the heel, and lifting or flexing the foot, so that the toe is up off the floor, you can catch back the toe by bending the knee quickly and pulling (or picking up) the toe tap. The action will give you a tap going *up and back*.

Exercise

Try this exercise. You must start with foot flat and rested without weight; let's say the R foot resting just apart and to the front of the L. The knee is slightly bent but by slowly straightening it you will do this hinge action just mentioned.

Keep this action going until only the heel is in contact with the floor and then continue until you 'catch back' the toe rising off the floor, up and back, by giving it a good hard pull (or 'pick') (pictures 11.5a–d).

You will have to repeat this several times to get it quite right so practise as much as possible but always beginning with the foot flat. Go through the same routine of: foot flat, knee bent; straighten knee slowly; lift the toe off the floor in a hinge motion, leaving heel in contact; bend the knee sharply, catching the toe tap on the floor in an upward and lifting action.

picture 11.5a Flat foot

picture 11.5b The hinge

picture 11.5c The 'catch'

picture 11.5d The pick-up

Try not to bring the foot behind you; rather try to keep it in front of you. But you can practise either one because they will both be used.

This must be a quick movement to avoid any 'wiping' action. Think of it like a stick on a drum – you beat downwards, but the upward reflex gives a different sound to the one you would hear if you had left the stick down for a moment. The toes have to almost bounce off the floor here!

In the absolute ideal you will flex twice, the first time in the hinge position and then instantaneously after the sound of the pick-up. The foot will be lifted in front and flexed at the ankle.

This picking up action is a backward action, like the tap-step is a forward action. Each of these is the reverse of itself. Landing the foot down on the ball will give you the pick-up step (or, if done without weight in that foot, a pick-up ball).

But, we never dance just forward and backward. We also dance sideways, and we also turn. So, if we do a forward tap-step say, we can also angle it to the side, while still technically doing a forward action. Try this now. Do a tap-step forward and then forward and to the side.

Your feet are now apart. By the same token we can do a pick-up to the side too, by again angling the action inwards. So, pick-up backward and inward to join the foot already out to the side. Do; R >>>, L >>>, R >>>, L >>>, going to the R side with a tap-step and pick-up step, but achieving a sideways travelling action in an opening and closing sequence of moves. This is an exercise for the tap-step and pick-up which will help our Shim Sham 3. It is only this inward action with the pick-up that we need here. The outward action can be just a single step on the ball. The 'joining' action by picking up lands on the ball too, without weight.

Right, that's enough of the exercises, let's do the … Shim Sham 3.

1. You are currently in the R foot because the Shim Sham 2 break ends on that foot (go back and remind yourself of this step and end it on the R). A simple weight transfer now into the L will begin our next Shim Sham.

2. Step on the ball with the L to the L side, hingeing the R, before doing a pick-up inward to close, landing on the ball without weight. Now, do the opposite – step the R to the R side (it's free because you didn't transfer weight into it) and hinge the L before doing a pick-up inward on that foot to close onto the ball without weight. Now repeat the L again, then the R again, like this:

   stp L to L side, p-up R and join with L........ '8 and 1'

   stp R to R side, p-up L and join with R........ '2 and 3'

   stp L to L side, p-up R and join with L........ '4 and 5'

   stp R to R side, p-up L and join with R........ '6 and 7'

On this very last L, you must change weight and do a ball-change R L (but using a stamp stamp would be better).

Listen to track 49 of the CD here for this double weight change L R L, and hear how the ball-change is quite heavy; that's why you can use two flats instead of ball and step. This will magnify what is an infectious change to give a really strong punch on the counts '<u>7 and 8</u>'. Of course, this '8' is the next 8 you will be repeating on, on the L foot again (pictures 11.6a–c).

picture 11.6a The hinge

picture 11.6b The catch

picture 11.6c The close

Count it so:

stp	p-upbl	stp	p-upbl	stp	p-upbl	stp	p-up	stp	flat-	(flat)
L	R	R	L	L	R	R	L	R		(L)
8	and1	2	and3	4	and5	6	and7	and		(8)

Repeat, but don't forget, do not change sides this time! Repeat twice.

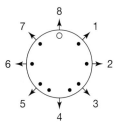

figure 11.7

Let me be quite clear – when you do this strong R L (on the two flats) you have made your first step (on the L on '8') of the next time. You have begun the next side, so carry on and repeat yourself.

Miss out the flat-flat on the third side and end on the '7' on the L. This is the 'and 7' above, on this third side. Now we can simply step into our break with the free R on the ball.

Count this third side as follows:

stp	p-upbl	stp	p-upbl	stp	p-upbl	stp	p-up	stp
L	R	R	L	L	R	R	L	
8	and 1	2	and 3	4	and 5	6	and 7	

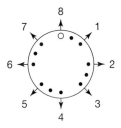

figure 11.8

The break

This is the easy part because you have done it already! Using the Shim Sham 1 break learnt earlier, step into that R foot on '8'. Now continue, which means the next thing will be the heel of the R and toe behind with the L. The counts are: '8 1 2', as before.

Now go on and do the two hop-steps, R-L, L-R (3 and and 5) and then the final two steps, L R on 6 7. This is the break from Shim Sham 1.

bl	hl	to	hp-stp	hp-stp	stp	stp
R	R	L	R–L	L-R	L	R (rest)
8	1	2	3 and __	and 5	6	7 __

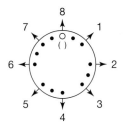

figure 11.9

The only difficulty in this step I think, is fitting in the pick-ups because they are quite hard to squeeze into such a small space. The inward pull takes a little getting used to, but don't forget this is *not* a beginners' step at this point, it is much more advanced. If you can master this and you have no experience, you are really doing well.

We may as well now try to do all three Shim Shams with, hopefully, the Shimmy going on a lot of the time, just to see how you get along.

We have come this far, so let's finish it all off with the Shim Sham 4.

Shim Sham 4

Use CD track 50.

Remember, there are variations of the Shim Sham, but the basic is the same. To do this last one traditionally, would be like so:

(I will assume your feet are together here, but the R is resting as before.)

1. Begin with weight on L, drop with a *flat foot* onto the R in front. Use a good full-bodied sound here, with weight right forward over the foot and with knee bent quite deeply (pictures 11.7a and b). Leave the L foot behind but off the floor. Transfer back into the L, on the ball, and come up a little from this deep knee bend. You are now in the L; do a shuffle ball-change on the R, out to the R side and landing behind the L on the ball. Change into the L, of course, here but onto a good *flat* sound.

picture 11.7a   Full-foot drop

picture 11.7b side view

3. Now, do the break from Shim Sham 1, for the break here – '8 1 2 3 and and 5 6 7' ball heel toe hop-step hop-step step step.

Repeating all of this on the same side will give you the traditional Shim Sham 4, which completes the whole 4 × 8s structure.

Of course, this contravenes the rule because it now only uses 1 × 8 and then 1 × 8 again, for the break before repeating. The other three Shim Sham use the 3 × 8s plus 1 × 8 break structure! Sorry, but I didn't invent this one!

In case that has confused: Shim Sham 1, 2 and 3 are all in 8s, using the standard three sides, each of 8 counts, and one side of 8 counts for the break. But not here – it is a case of 'do one side and then break' and repeat. Makes the whole thing more interesting. But, I did say there are variations! So, here's mine coming up!

Hartley's Shim Sham 4

Having done the first three Shim Shams as described, this variation is on number 4 only and it's really quite simple.

Okay, here we go, and count it in 8s, to keep them all the same. Try this with track 51 on the CD.

2. Do this twice on the same foot, really accenting the flats. The rhythm is: <u>8</u> 1 and 2 and <u>3</u>; <u>4</u> 5 and 6 and <u>7</u>. See figure 11.10.

drp	stp	shfl	bl-ch;	drp	stp	shfl	bl-ch
R	L	R	R-L;	R	L	R	R-L
<u>8</u>	<u>1</u> and 2 and 3;			<u>4</u>	<u>5</u> and 6 and 7		

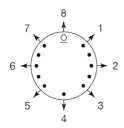

figure 11.10

1. Drop as before on the R, forward and with a flat foot, leaving the L behind and off the floor. Transfer back into the L on the ball; do the shuffle ball-change on the R, as before. Do this twice, using 8 counts. See figure 11.11.

drp	stp	shfl	bl-ch;	drp	stp	shfl	bl-ch
R	L	R	R-L;	R	L	R	R-L
<u>8</u>	<u>1</u>	and 2	and 3;	<u>4</u>	<u>5</u>	and 6	and 7

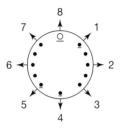

figure 11.11

2. The weight is now in the L. Then do the first one of Shim Sham 2 – easy! This will take you to the other side, and use the same count as Shim Sham 2: 8 1 2 3 4 5and __ and 7. See figure 11.12.

stamp	bl	stamp	bl	stp	hl-bl	hl-bl
R	L	R	L	R	R-L	L-R
8	1	2	3	4	5 and __	and 7

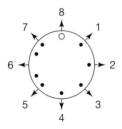

figure 11.12

Count them both so: (figures 11.11 and 11.12)

8 1 and 2 and 3; 4 5 and 6 and 7

8 1 2 3 4 5 and __ and 7 (Shim Sham 2)

3. You're on the R foot, having done the R side using the Shim Sham 2 to get here.

4. Now, on the L do the crossover break from the Shim Sham 2.

(8 1 and ___ and 3; 4 5 and ___ and 7). See figure 11.13.

stp	hl-bl		hl-bl	stp	hl-bl	hl-bl
L	L-R		R-L	R	R-L	L-R
8	1 and	___	and3	4	5and ___	and7

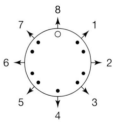

figure 11.13

5. Then we can do my syncopated ending, using the weaving pattern we did in the combination to *Anything Goes*. Also, it's almost identical in rhythm. See figure 11.14.

stp	hl-bl		hl-bl	hl-bl		hl-bl	stp
L	L-R		R-L	R-L		L-R	R
8	1 and	___	a 3	4 and	___	a 6	7....perfect!

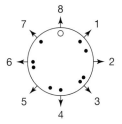

figure 11.14

That's the Hartley Shim Sham 4 all done!

You have achieved so much if you are here, and began reading this book as a beginner! So much, I can't tell you. If you have grasped all of the preceding instructions, counts and steps you have truly come a long way.

If you were not a beginner when you started this book you will by now, have learnt a lot about another style that perhaps you were not familiar with. As I explained earlier this is not a syllabus style, but rather just my own way of doing things. Well, hey, the syllabus style is already in print, right?

picture 11.8   Doing it my way!

12 other famous steps

In this chapter you will learn:

- much more than the basics
- how to strain your brain
- what tap dancers go through.

12

These steps are essential to further learning and even if you have just dipped into this book and landed on this page, you will get an explanation at least, of some of the great steps from history. For example, what on earth is a Cramp Roll? It is certainly on our list …

● Paddles

● Riffs

● Cramp rolls

● Double pull-back

● Pick-up on one foot

● Train step

● Buffalo

● Scissors and One

● Suzie Q

● Maxie Ford

Now that we have come this far I want to introduce you to a few of the more famous steps you will come across if you continue with this quest to tap dance. They sometimes have pretty slick names. Read on.

Paddles

Paddles have already been explained in Chapter 07 and are absolutely essential to this style. They are from a mixture of sources and its impossible to ascertain where some steps originated, and from whom. It is easy to see from the paddle's earthy nature that it's a step of African origin because it is definitely floor bound. A black, rhythm tap style does not use paddles exclusively but they figure greatly.

If we use the other major staple step, the Shuffle, we can see the similarities and I hope to get you switching between the two at will. However, there is a small problem. I have done a good job on you to really flex that ankle on the Shuffle but now, I want you to keep the ankle in a fixed position to do the paddle. Only work from the knee.

When I first came across paddles (within ten minutes of meeting my teacher I realized I could not tap! And I had been 'tapping' for years! This one step convinced me I had to begin again) I was taken aback. It was such a simple thing to see and hear but I couldn't see where all the sound was coming from! Paddles are tricky at first and even advanced dancers, if they haven't seen them before, have initial problems. Have patience.

Paddles then, are *the* basic ingredient of black Rhythm Tap and because they are so low to the floor, can take you to great speed. They can be done large or, once mastered, appear to be miniscule as the technique for doing them gets refined more and more. Eventually the whole shoe is almost like a spinning disc as it works from the ankle; it becomes a roll in the ankle and not just a simple forward and backward action like the shuffle.

Because it doesn't lift at the knee at this later stage it can go much faster than a shuffle – there is simply less involved.

The paddle is the heel and toe action explained in Chapter 07. When you add the ball and heel of the same foot and arrive at this iconic step, its called a paddle and roll. We will call this a four-beat paddle (4bt pdl). You will discover this exquisite step, as I did, with amazement! Paddle and roll is the original name for this four-beat sound and it is a derivative of a 'paradiddle', which is a drummer's term for a quick four-sound action using two hands and two sticks, with each closely linked. Each hand will do a double hit, picking up speed as they progress. You can say it yourself: 'para-diddle' ('1 and 2 and'); 'para-diddle' ('1 and 2 and'). As fast as you can go with your hands here, the feet can go faster with the paddle and roll. By the way, why are these simple things barely featured in any English syllabus and when they are, why are they labelled 'advanced'?

Refer back to Chapter 07, section Paddles now and go over the technique to doing them. Add the ball-heel every time and thus do paddle and roll for half an hour, to see how your speed can increase.

Okay, back to the four-beat paddle. Here we can also investigate the three-beat, five-beat, six-beat, seven-beat and eight-beat paddle and roll. Listen to CD tracks 25 to 29.

> **Remember:**
>
> Do large for slow and small for fast. Count it in various ways: '1 and and a'; 'and 1 and 2'; 'and and a 1'; '1 and a 2', etc.

> **Good point!**
>
> You know, in my beginners' classes I can get even the first-timers to give me at least five sounds in one second! Just think of that for a moment – five sounds in one movement of the clock. Very good? And in an advanced class people can regularly and easily do between 16 and 20! Incredible? However, complacency disappears when I mention the world record is around 32! In one second. Unbelievable? Yes, but it's official, so . . .

For the three-beat paddle (3bt pdl), just stay on the ball when landing; don't put the heel down. You can count these in various ways too, but for now use the rhythm that goes with our three sounds – 'and a 1' or '1 and a'. This will look and feel like a shuffle-step, so we can call this paddle-step; don't forget, landings are on the ball every time.

For the five-beat paddle (5bt pdl), we must add something to the four beat, for example add a heel beat in the middle of the four. Do: paddle...heel...step-heel like so:

pdl hl stp-hl;   pdl hl stp-hl

 R   L   R ;   L   R   L

You can count these 'a 1 and a 2'. Or '1 and and a 2'. Or 'a 1 and 2 and'. There are five sounds here, of course, so it's more versatile, especially because it's an odd number of sounds across a usually even rhythm.

This is a very special paddle and roll because of its dexterity. You can begin with the heel dig (normal paddle) or the new middle heel. But it is further dextrous when you experiment with the counts. The permutations are endless with this step. Of course, when you can constantly switch from 3 to 4 to 5 to 4 to 3 to 5 to 4 to 3, you can become master of rhythm far beyond the fundamental. With paddles you can set up rolling rhythms that can go on for many bars of music and be rather interesting and complex. Rather like a piano roll or fingering on a guitar fingerboard, it's possible to achieve advanced rhythmic connections with relatively little movement. It's all from the ankle once you have mastered it, and fairly tireless for the body.

The six-beat paddle (6bt pdl) will add further possibilities. Do the first paddle on the R (heel and toe), heel on the L. Then tap-step heel on the R, changing weight into it. Repeat both sides and count it '1 and 2 and 3 and', or 'and 1 and 2 and 3'. Keeping to this even count gives less of a headache while learning the paddles and it makes a clever, but easy, sound.

The seven-beat paddle (7bt pdl) is a good example of the mixing of styles. You will be using shuffles and paddles. Do again the first paddle on the R, then heel L followed by shuffle step-heel R. Repeat both sides and count it '1 and 2 and 3 and 4'.

The eight-beat paddle (8bt pdl) is again using shuffles as well as paddles and, because it gives you more time within the step, feels very comfortable to do. Do a paddle on the R in front; a heel on the L. Then a shuffle to the R side on the R; heel L, again in place. Finish with a step-heel on the R, but slightly behind the L. This has automatically placed the L in front to begin again.

Count it so:

pdl hl shfl hl stp hl

R L R L R R

1 and 2 and 3 and 4 and

Do this R and L and keep it running; build up a speed.

Major point:

Here, we could re-cap our elemental approach. We have: shuffles, heels, paddles, step-heels, paddle-heels, shuffle-heels, even shuffle heel step-heel. I am hoping you recognize all of these terms by now!

Count the eight-beat paddle so:

Evenly: 1 and 2 and 3 and 4 and .... for the R side

Evenly: 5 and 6 and 7 and 8 and .... for the L side

Equally, begin on 'and 1' with the first heel of the paddle and do the full even eight counts that way. This step should give you great satisfaction and in no time your speed will increase. Keep the rhythm in even 8th notes.

Try now to mix these paddles in the following examples: all counting is even. Change feet on every number, e.g. 3(beat paddle) on the R; 4(beat paddle) on the L alternating.

3 4 5 3 4 5 8   begin on the even count 'and 1'

8 4 4 8 4 4 5 6 6 7 7   begin on the even count '1'

5 5 3 3 5 5 3 3 4 4 8 4 4 8   begin on 'and 1'

String them along, changing the numbers as you change feet. Your aim is to get a rolling sound, and streams of beats with *no* discernable break, pause or gap.

Do all of this and the door has opened for you on a whole new plane of tap dancing.

Riffs

A riff is a walking step or a step that moves you along. It's most simply explained as 'multiple sounds from a single action' – the action of the leg swinging through from front to back – er, that's walking. Listen to CD tracks 30 to 34 for this section.

There are, as with paddles, three-, four-, five-, six- and seven-beat riffs and I will describe them as follows:

The three-beat riff (3bt rf) can be either walking or not but the riff itself is a brush with the toe and heel, one after the other. Starting with the foot behind, bring it through, striking and brushing the toe tap and flexing the ankle so that the heel brushes immediately after it. You will have two very close sounds, with the rhythm usually 'and 1'.

Do the first sound of the toe brushing but then hit the heel down onto the   floor (not brushing as before but digging) and follow this with the toe beating into the floor with a strong change of weight. You end with the foot completely flat now as you transfer. You will hear '1 and 2' or 'and a 1'. You should develop this into a walking action.

The four-beat riff (4bt rf) begins the same as the first three-beat riff, with the toe and heel brushing forward. Do this and then put the heel directly down where it falls naturally after the swing through from the knee. Now put the toe down and transfer weight. It's 'two beats up, two beats down'. Or, two off and two on if you see. The leg should go through a straight position on the walk and land where it comes down, on the heel.

Try it out using just your R foot, then your L, a few times repeatedly.

Now do it over again and *add a heel beat* on the other foot. You have now done 'and a 1', a really close triplet, with the foot still in the air, flexed and held in front. You have not moved from the spot, but you can move if you now do the three-beat riff the second way.

picture 12.1a   The five-beat riff …   **picture 12.1b**   – Beat 1

picture 12.1c   – Beat 2   **picture 12.1d**   **picture 12.1e**   – Beat 3

picture 12.1f – Beat 4

picture 12.1g – Beat 5

Don't forget, try to walk always, by keeping it all flowing as well as you can. Walk in a sensible stride, not too far but also not too close either.

The seven-beat riff (7bt rf) is my favourite of all and it couldn't be simpler. It is, of course, the five plus two beats; this time the extras are two heels again but they will be done 'back, front' after completing the five-beat riff. Again, as with the six-beat riff, the last sound must obviously be on the foot doing the riff.

Try this fascinating step that you can do just with a walk. Tap is made up of countless riffs like this one and a little practice will find great speed quite soon. I like to do these little steps on the beat as well as off, so you could count this: '1 and a 2'; '1 and and a' ; 'and and a 1'. The usual way is also valid and that is 'a 1 a 2'.

The next follows on from this and it's the five-beat riff (5bt rf). It is almost identical to the five-beat paddle, where the added beat is in the middle of the four beats. On this premise then, do a four-beat riff but put an extra heel in the middle – the first two beats up, then a heel on the other foot, then the rest of the riff, heel landing first followed by the toe beat down to transfer weight.

It counts: 'a 1 and a 2; a 3 and a 4', etc. A good speed can be created here because the technique can be worked upon with ease. You don't need too much room but it is a moving step. See Pictures 12.1a–g.

For the six-beat riff (6bt rf) the process is easier and thus it's only a question of adding one to the end of the five-beat riff; therefore, do the five and add an extra heel right at the end. You will do: the first two beats up, the 'a' heel on the other foot, then the rest of the riff, heel landing first followed by toe beat down, and then the heel on the same foot.

You can count this: 'a1 a2 a3'; 'and 1 and 2 and 3'; 'and a 1 and a 2'.

Don't forget these are walking steps and all riffs transfer.

Cramp rolls

These are perhaps the quickest steps of all because they are just so tiny. They are under the foot's own weight and consist of beats cramped into one count. We can do four- or five- beat cramps rolls (4/5 bt crmp rl), and with very little effort sound very capable. With a single spring down into the floor, we can do four or five very fast sounds using the following:

- ball-ball-heel-heel (R-L-R-L) for the four-beat cramp.
- tap-step-ball-heel-heel (R-R-L-R-L) for the five-beat cramp.

These quick sounds are in one count and therefore must be counted like so; 'and and a 1' for the four-beat and 'and and and a 1' for the five-beat.

Cramp rolls are great for that unexpected and effortless input while in the middle of a routine or a flowing step, consisting of say, just normal shuffles and paddles. They can be done with feet together, feet apart, crossing – and when you become a soloist, they can be turning too! Later, I will introduce a couple of these into the routines we will attempt together.

Double pull-back

This flashy step uses a lot of energy and achieves the same sound as the four-beat riff and, actually, the four-beat cramp. It is initially four beats but it can be added to, as always, by putting in extra sounds. But, of course, these extras must be attached so that it all sounds like one move. So, to do a six-beat pull-back, you could land on the balls of the feet and then put down the two heels, to make six beats.

However, to do this we will have to do a series of exercises to get into the swing. It is not a step that will just happen, it will take time and give hours of pleasure once achieved. It requires energy and flair but most of all patience.

Begin with weight on both feet and with the R slightly in front of the L. The R foot will move first, followed immediately by the L. With a very quick action spring back with a very small step on the R and the L. They will sound 'a 1' and you have landed on the balls of both feet, one after the other; the heels at this point are still lifted. Do this exercise again and again to get speed and power into the floor, via two short, sharp movements.

The other part of this pull back section is the harder to master, but we will try it now.

What has to happen is that on the way up from the knees flexed position, the toes coming off the floor must catch the floor before landing. We have already done the landings, but on the way we have to squeeze in the pull-backs. Doing two of them will give our double pull-back (dbl pl-bk)!

Try to do this exercise first:

Exercise

Stand behind a chair with your hands resting on the chair back. Support your weight off the floor sufficiently to do a picking up/pulling back action on both feet. Leaning over the chair you can probably do this on each foot in turn for a 'pick-up on one foot' action, but you can certainly do this on both feet at once, landing on the balls.

Try to do this each foot in turn, doing a lift-off from one foot, then trying to catch the toe tap before landing on the ball of that foot. Using the chair to help with the lift should accommodate the pick-up (pictures 12.2a and b).

Obviously now you have to do this from a standing position, without the chair, and with the feet as described, one in front of the other. Bend the knees and just bounce and flex both of them, getting yourself ready to do this double lift-off. Get into the floor, still with both feet flat and, when ready, spring backwards, bringing off one foot then the other *but* catching the toe tap of each foot with a pick-up action. You will take off from a flat foot but when the knees straighten and you lift off from the floor the toes will come up just enough to catch before they land again.

picture 12.2a   R foot is flat on the floor

picture 12.2b Landing after the pick-up

Pick-up on one foot

I should say here, are you ready? Because this *will* be a workout, I can promise you. You could regard it as just that, or you could become so good at it you could use it in the many hours of dance you will be doing one day. Here we go.

Stand on one foot – probably your favourite foot – and practise hopping. A few points to remember here: keep the weight forward and land on a good strong bent knee; don't hop up, but hop *down* into the floor with a short sharp action; land on the ball of foot only.

Now, try hopping backwards and in a multiple set of exercises to build some strength. This may sound strange, but it's all going towards the action of picking up on one foot. Remember also this is not a beginners' step, but one of those famous steps that you may see and want to do later, yourself. Many steps are quite difficult and any skill learnt will become gradually harder then gradually more fulfilling. When you do this hop backwards, stay as low as you can.

You are trying to lift off the floor but also to fit in a beat on the way! That beat is the pick-up on one foot and it must now start from a flat foot as your preparation. It will probably not come for quite some time and you may need your chair again – I would use it to begin with anyway. Keep your weight over it and practise the hop low and backwards. Eventually you will fit in this pick-up and land on the ball. Restart each one now from a flat foot. The landing is as shown in picture 12.2b.

Good luck again with this strength-building workout.

If you could do this in slow motion you would see a pick-up, pick-up, land, land (R, L, R, L), that is both pick-ups before both landings; it is, of course, slightly difficult to stay in the air!

The sound is quick and counts like a cramp roll, i.e. four beats in one count, and is 'and and a 1' or '1 and and a'. You need to feel like you are pulling the toes off the floor but with an additional sound from each one, before landing on each one again. Good luck in this workout!

Train step

This is a crossover step, which, because it's easily learnt, quickly picks up speed and naturally sounds like a train pulling away. It isn't really called a train step but it's such a good description we can leave it as it is.

The step consists of three steps and three sounds, and I always imagine it in a triangle shape, with one large point in the front of two smaller ones in the back. The large point in front is a stamp (with weight) and the two behind are balls of foot. See pictures 12.3a–e.

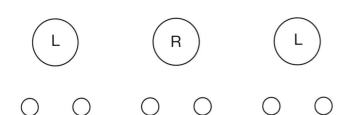

figure 12.1

A change of weight is required on every step, with a 'heavy, light, light' effect – front, back, back. Step on the imaginary circle in figure 12.1.

Stamp on the R and change weight L, R into the other two feet; this will automatically put you on the L side, with a repeat stamp on the L, followed by the next two steps R, L, which will then automatically put you on the R side, with a stamp – well, you get the message.

Count it in two ways. First: in the twelfth musical mode (see Chapter 08 Rhythm and counting explained), which will be '1 and a', and thus with the stamp always occurring on the strong down beat or the actual number.

It will sound the stamp emphasis every time the same, like so:

<u>1</u> and a <u>2</u> and a <u>3</u> and a <u>4</u> and a <u>5</u> and a <u>6</u> and a <u>7</u> and a <u>8</u>

picture 12.3a   Train step begins

picture 12.3b   First stamp across

Second, count in the even eighth mode (see same chapter on Rhythm) which will now have the steps cross-phrasing, to give a sort of moving emphasis. The stamp will land on the number and the next time on an 'and', followed by the next time on a number, and the next time on an 'and'. Here is our syncopation again, when the stresses or emphases shift along, to land alternately on different parts of the rhythm. It is what makes tap dance, well – tap dance!

- Trap the following counts in your head and say the <u>underlined</u> parts louder.

- Clap the rhythm, using the underlined to clap louder.
- Tap the rhythm with the feet, using the shape given – one large point, two small points.

You can hopefully feel this changing or moving stress. If you tend to speed up, you're doing the train step – don't forget to whistle!

picture 12.3c   Going to the other foot

picture 12.3d   Next stamp across

picture 12.3e Going to the other foot

Buffalo

This is a traditional step and somewhat dated in my opinion. However, you could say that about the time step and other steps. It has the old 'stage look' about it so therefore it's a legitimate thing to learn, even if the place for it in a dance would be to add a nostalgic touch.

It travels to either L or R side, and looks quite neat and smart once it is practised, but it does require practice. Put on track 35 of the CD.

Begin with weight on the L; hop on L and do a shuffle step on the R, but landing across, *behind the L and turned out*. When you land this foot, exaggerate the lift of the L in front (picture 12.4).

Now you have freed the L. Do a tap-step on this L foot out to the side and do another shuffle step crossing behind on the R, again exaggerating the transfer of weight. This crossing and lifting behind and in front gives the step its unique 'Buffalo look'.

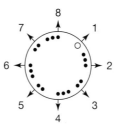

figure 12.2

Keep repeating this to get the following count:

(after the initial hop to get started, all first steps will be tap-step)

hp	shfl-stp	tp-stp	shfl-stp	tp-stp	shfl-stp	tp-stp	shfl-stp
L	R	L	R	L	R	L	R
1	and a 2	a3	and a 4	a5	and a 6	a7	and a 8

Scissors and One

This is my own name for a step that Fred Astaire himself uses in one of his films. I am sure he didn't call it Scissors and One but there you go, I have!

You have actually already done this step earlier; it is the *shuffle ball-change*. Here, though, I want you to do a *spring* shuffle ball-change. This will obviously mean you doing five sounds on each side, i.e. spring shuffle ball-change to the L side; spring shuffle ball-change to the R side – and so on.

The five sounds here are to be done in a simple line of: 1 2 3 4 5. In other words, do not assume any rhythm at the moment, but rather just do the sounds equally. If we do both sides following each other we will have ten sounds; count it: '1and 2 and 3 and 4 and 5 and'.

You may have guessed already – *an odd number of sounds per side, but an even number of beats in our rhythm*.

This is another cross-phrasing exercise, when the stresses move around and the rhythm gets interesting. But why is it called Scissors and One?

picture 12.4   Drop into R

picture 12.5a The spring

picture 12.5b The landing: crossed position

When you spring onto, say, the L, you must spring to the L side and do the shuffle ball-change to the R side, landing this in a crossed position; L behind R. Repeat to the other side, with the same actions, landing R behind L on the ball-change and gain some flow in the execution. It should almost feel like bouncing from side to side. This crossing and changing action is called 'scissoring'. See pictures 12.5a–c to get the idea of this scissor effect. I hope you can understand the concept of this action.

If you can grasp this quite advanced step, well done. If you already know the step, you will know not to group the rhythm by doing 'a1 and a 2' or '1 and and a 2'. No, this figure is actually a shuffle ball-change plus *one* other sound, which is the spring, on each side repeating. If you are doing it with this scissor action you have the step Scissors and One – and I could be very proud of you right now!

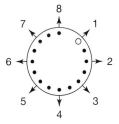

figure 12.3

Count it so:

spr	shfl	bl-ch	spr	shfl	bl-ch	spr	shfl	bl-ch
L	R	R-L	R	L	L-R	L	R	R-L
1	and2	and 3	and	4and	5 and	6	and7	and 8

It can be done very fast and it can go forward or backward or stay on the spot. Of course, it can be small or large too. Try to master this simple but effective step. And, if you would like to see how it is *really* done, rent or buy the Fred Astaire film *Second Chorus* and watch him as he leads the orchestra. Be amazed.

picture 12.5c   The other landing on ball-change

Suzie Q

Here is another step from the archives, a good looking step to do and enjoy. It may be seen in lots of routines of the nostalgic variety but I don't think I have seen it often in a film.

All right, here we go. Two things must happen at once here, and the effect is to give a dynamic look because it's all going on at the same time.

Do a hard downward step into the floor with the L to the L side and at the same time open the R to the side, with a straight knee to get the foot hingeing upwards and outwards, and leaving the heel in contact with the floor (picture 12.6a).

picture 12.6a   Step down hard and hinge the R

Land on the flat all the time because it is easier and don't forget it repeats to *one side only*. To do the other side, pause and change direction.

You are now doing step pick-up flat, step pick-up flat, step pick-up flat and counting '1 a2, 3 a4, 5 a6, 7 a8'.

Well done!

Maxie Ford

This is very similar to the Scissors and One step above. The difference is that it is a grouped beat step and unlike the Scissors and One it is not a continuous flow kind of step. Rather it is an explosive thing that has lots going on but with a single initial action.

Also, I must explain it is not an easy step to do and may take a while to achieve. Like the double pull-back, explained earlier, it is an example of a step that will arrive

picture 12.6b   The landing

Practise this a few dozen times, just stepping down hard and flexing the other ankle. By doing the step with a forceful action, it sort of frees the other foot fractionally quicker.

Now that your R foot is angled up and out to the R side it is ready to pull in with an inward pick-up action before landing on the flat next to the L. Now step again and repeat the action as many times as you like. You will find that you travel to the L side because your feet are opening and closing. The rhythm will be '1 a2'; '3 a4', and so on.

What has to happen now is that the closing foot must land down in front of the other foot and turned in (picture 12.6b). This will result in an *opening and crossing* action taking place, and having the effect of looking like more is actually going on than there is.

picture 12.7a   Drop and shuffle

picture 12.7b   Landing on ball

at your feet only with a great deal of practise; and is another explosive step that you may have done in the past. Try doing this to track 36 of the CD.

Do a quick and full foot landing (drop) on the L and to the L side and lift off the R and prepare to shuffle it and bring it in towards the L. Your R is in a lifted position because you are in the L and with R off the floor. Practise this action a lot to get the sound to be: '1 and a'; '2 and a', and so on. To do the next action – a pick-up – from this set position will be hard. The answer is to do the two things together – this will be the whole point of the step anyway! Listen to track 37 of the CD.

So, what will happen is: drop on the L (1); shuffle on the R (a2) (picture 12.7a); pick-up on the L (and); land on the ball of the R followed by the L, also on the ball (a 3). You should be in a crossed-over position because you have done a scissor-like action with L going behind the R to land on the ball (picture 12.7b). The count is very interesting because it goes: '1 a2 and a3'. (A famous tap teacher I know does not teach with counts – she teaches with words. But, her words are very much her own! How can anyone understand this: 'bap de diddly bap'? But she is a great teacher from the USA and her name is Brenda Bufalino.)

You are now in the L so you can do the same thing on the other side. Land with a drop on the R (4); shuffle on the L (a5); pick-up on the R l(and); land on the ball of the L followed by the R (a6).

The count is now: 1 a2 and a 3, 4 a5 and a 6. All that remains is to step on the balls of each foot, L and R, to get to the end of our 8 counts – 7, 8.

As I stated, this is a scissor-like action, going from side to side. It is an effective initial action step that sort of springs from foot to foot by landing and using this dynamic. A drop is a dynamic and is used to lift the speed of the next thing you are doing. It also counts only as we have done here and this count is part of its appeal and history; everybody who tap dances knows this step and loves to do it.

It can be difficult, as I mentioned, at first; it's quite hard to stay in the air practising something that will require you to go through the air. Try to practise, then, using the whole action. This will help, I feel, because it builds up the confidence and the speed of execution will produce the step. Do one, then do the other side, and link them together to produce the famous Maxie Ford.

My Point (of view):

Sometimes this book may appear to be for more than the beginner, and this is how I have decided it should be. At this point that is definitely the case! When I began the book I had to remember that it was *you*, the novice tap dancer, that I was speaking to. However, I realized after a short while that you may not be a beginner, but rather someone who has tap danced before, long ago. You may even be a teacher! You may want to see if those feelings can be regained somehow, preferably from where you left off five, ten, fifteen, twenty-nine years ago, yes? Well, that could indeed happen if we are getting along.

Therefore, I am deliberately including much more information – about styles, harder steps, ways with rhythm and so on – in an effort to both inform and entertain. It will be a familiar feeling for many, to go over steps and things that they once knew, and I hope I have so far helped with any recapture of lost youth! If you are reading this for the first time and are up with the level of the book so far, you must be feeling quite proud of yourself by now.

We have come quite a long way down the tap dance road and could probably use some easy and comfortable (and small) combinations to see how we are doing, sort of like a mid-term test. So, let's try this short combination, which can be danced to track 52 of the CD.

Combination 1

Use CD track 52.

Look out for a heel-brush (hl-br), which is the action of brushing the heel, as you learnt to do with the toe tap earlier.

tp-stp	tp-stp	tp-stp	bl-ch	tp-stp	tp-stp	tp-stp	bl-ch
R	L	R	L-R	L	R	L	R-L
a1	a2	a3	a4	a5	a6	a7	a8

figure 12.4

hp   shfl-stp   tp-stp   shfl-stp   tp-stp   shfl-stp   tp-stp   shfl-stp...to L

(...Buffalo...)

L   R   L   R   L   R   L   R

1   and a 2   a3   and a 4   a5   and a 6   a7   and a 8

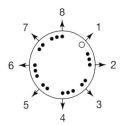

figure 12.5

kick stp stp hl-br hl ... to R;   stp   stp stp hl-br hl...to L

L   L   R   L   R   L   R   L   R   L

1   2   3   and 4   5   6   7   and 8

(kick the L low out to L side and bring it round behind the R to travel to the R side. Then go to L side)

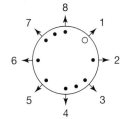

figure 12.6

stp   stp   shfl stp-hl   pdl stp-hl   bl-hl

R   L   R   L   R

1   2   a3 a4   a5 a6   a7   ___

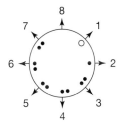

figure 12.7

Trap, Clap, Tap here ...

Combination 2

Look at figures 12.8–12.13 for the rhythms here.

Combination 2 uses more from our 'famous steps' section. Refer to track 53 of the CD.

Train step, beginning R. Remember stamp ball ball.

<u>1</u> and 2 <u>and</u> 3 and <u>4</u> and 5 <u>and</u> 6 and <u>7</u>

R L R L R L   R L R L R L R

tp-stp   p-up stp   stp to the L side

and 8   and a   1

L   R   L

4bt pdl   4bt pdl   4bt crmp rl   R stp

R   L   R   R

2 and a 3   4 and a 5   6 and and a   7

Next – **Shim Sham 3.**

stamp stamp p-upbl stp p-upbl stp p-upbl stp p-up stp

L   R   L-L   L   R-R   R   L-L   L   R-R

and   8   a1   2   a3   4   a5   6   and 7

Repeat same side.

Next, **a single time step** (include the break) but ... help ... on the left side!

See if you can now refer back to the time step section and do just the single with the break. Good luck!

That should be 6 × 8s in all and sincere hopes are with you to do them all.

For the first time I am going to write down the rhythms by diagram only and in one continuous line. Here we go:

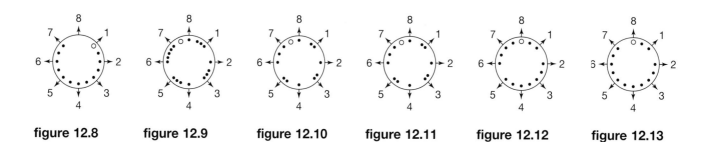

figure 12.8 figure 12.9 figure 12.10 figure 12.11 figure 12.12 figure 12.13

Trap, Clap, Tap

Combination 3

Refer to track 54 of the CD for this combination.

shfl	shfl	**5bt rf**		shfl	shfl	**5bt rf**
R	R	R		L	L	L
a1	a2	a3 and a 4		a5	a6	a7 and a 8

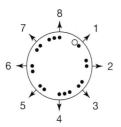

figure 12.14

4bt crmp rl	shfl	bl-ch	clap		**4bt crmp rl**	shfl	bl-ch	clap
	R	R	R-L			R	R	R-L
and and a 1	a2	a3	<u>and</u>	_	and and a 5	a6	a7	<u>and</u> _

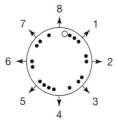

figure 12.15

(Scissors and One)

spr	shfl	stp	stp	spr	shfl	stp	stp	spr	shfl	stp
R	L	L	R	L	R	R	L	R	L	L
1	and 2	and	3	and 4	and	5	and	6	and 7	and __

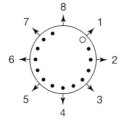

figure 12.16

Shim Sham 1 Break on the R and on 8:

bl	hl	to	hp-stp		hp-stp	stp	stp
R	R	L	R-L		L-R	L	R
8	1	2	3and	__	and 5	6	7

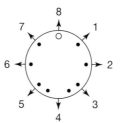

figure 12.17

shfl	hp-stp	shfl	bl-ch	stp		stp	bl-ch	bl-ch
L	R-L	R	R-L	R		L	R-L	R-L
a8	a1	a2	a3	and	__	5	a6	a7

stp	shfl	bl-ch	stp		stp	stp	
L	R	R-L	R		L	R	
1	a2	a3	4	__	6	7	__

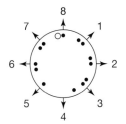

figure 12.18

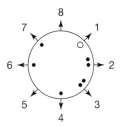

figure 12.21

dbl pl-bk		stp	stp	shfl	stp-hl	stp		
R		R	L	R	R-R	L		
8 and a 1		2	3	a4	and a	5	__	__

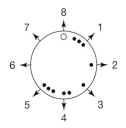

figure 12.19

This concludes the section on famous steps, but of course there are lots more. Some steps are created by simply doing the addition system that I have pursued all along. Following from that, you could even create your own mini combo! Good luck with that.

Trap, Clap, Tap

Use also the **Relax, Remind, Rewind** and **Repeat** mantra for yourself. Remember, it is brain game to tap dance.

shfl	hp-stp	shfl	bl-ch	stp		stp	bl-ch	bl-ch
R	L-R	L	L-R	L		R	L-R	L-R
a8	a1	a2	a3	and	__	5	a6	a7

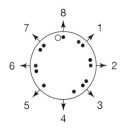

figure 12.20

amalgamations 13

In this chapter you will learn:

- musical style
- the joy of achievement
- that you're now tap dancing.

I must offer my congratulations to you if you have come to this point. If you are a beginner and have understood this book and its myriad instructions, well done – really well done! If you are re-reading or re-learning, and have enjoyed going through well-known steps *and* the style differences, I must thank you for buying the book and staying with it to learn to tap dance again.

Track list

55 Amalgamation 1

56 Amalgamation 2

57 Amalgamation 3

This chapter will help you to realize the potential of the diagrams and the knowledge of steps, and the idea of putting them together at the same time, rather like a song is learnt. The words and the music are learnt together, so we will (together) learn to do the two things at once.

The music on tracks 55, 56 and 57 of the CD resembles songs and tunes I have used for many years as I believe that dancing to a familiar tune is much easier than not doing so. Although the CD has original pieces on it I hope you can familiarize yourself with them to the extent that they are easy to dance to. If you have a piece or song you think sounds quite like them, please use it in conjunction. It is important you learn almost to 'absorb' the steps and music.

Following is my attempt at justifying the book and its methods to have you tap dancing. Tap is a solo dance, of course, but it is also a class dance with a great feeling of togetherness when everyone is dancing at the top of their game to the same piece of music. It is quite a thing to dance with sound coming from your own feet and feeling you are at one with yourself and your rhythm.

Try to give these steps and amalgamations some serious thought before you start. Explaining them in this way is done to hopefully get across not only steps but also *style*. The amalgamations are dance routines that require you to be more visual, so have patience – we are stepping out now!

Use the **Trap, Clap, Tap** method and get the rhythm into your head. Remember you have to have it there before you can get it to your feet. Sit down and go over the instructions and:

- **Relax** into the thought of dancing
- **Remind** yourself why you are doing it
- **Rewind** the whole set of instructions
- **Repeat** the routine to make you happy.

I sincerely hope you succeed with this method.

Amalgamation 1

picture 13.1a   Flap on R

picture 13.1b   Flap on L

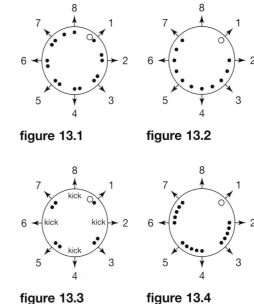

figure 13.1   figure 13.2

figure 13.3   figure 13.4

1. Beginning with R, do 7 flps going forward to the rhythm in figure 13.1.

   Then bl-ch L-R, on the count 'and 8' (pictures 13.1a and b).

2. Stp L on the bl to L side (1), and do a stp R over L (2), then stp L in place (and), R out to R side (3). This will count '1 2 and 3' (pictures 13.2a and b).

3. Repeat the last part of step 2 two more times to get the running rhythm '1 2 and 3 and 4 and 5 and 6 and 7'. Clap on 8 and at the same time kick the L out and over the R (see picture 13.3 and figure 13.2).

4. Bl-ch L-R (a1) then kick L in front and clap on this kick (2). Count it: 'a 1 2'.

5. Repeat this three more times to achieve the rhythm 'a1 2 a3 4 a5 6 and 7' but stop on '7'. This is kick bl-ch, kick bl-ch, kick bl-ch with a clap on the kick every time. (See pictures 13.3 and 13.4, and figure 13.3.)

picture 13.2b   Weight crossing into R

picture 13.2a   Weight change into R

6. Stp L (1); do 4bt pdl R, stamp L. Count it: '1 2 and and a 3'.

7. Repeat the 4bt pdl and stamp two more times. Your count now is: '1 2 and and a 3, 4 and and a 5, 6 and and a 7' (figure 13.4). You should have ended this in the L, with the R free to continue. See figures 13.1 to 13.4 for the rhythms.

8. Try now to do a triple time step, but *not* the break, starting with a shfl on the R and counting as normally '8 and'. To remind you, and so that you can compare to the diagram, the rhythm for a triple is: '8 and <u>1</u> and a <u>2</u> and 3 <u>and</u> ; 4 and <u>5</u> and a 6 and 7 <u>and</u>'. (See figure 13.5.)

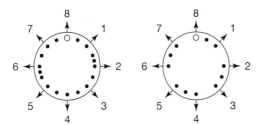

figure 13.5   **figure 13.6**

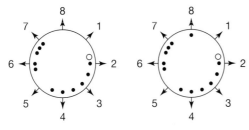

figure 13.7   **figure 13.8**

9. Do the Suzie Q, going to the R side, beginning with a stp (R), and hingeing the L up and out to the L side, ready to do your p-up (L). Do this p-up and stp the L across the R.

10. The counts are '8 and 1 2 and 3 4 and 5 6 and 7'. (See picture 13.6.) You are now in your L, and crossed over the R.

picture 13.3   Kick

picture 13.4   Ball change

11. Now do a toe (tip of your shoe) on the R, immediately followed by a hl on the L and on the count of 'a2'. This will be very rapid and is counted 'a2'; you have *waited* for the counts '8, 1'. (See figure 13.7.)

picture 13.5   Cross over for Suzie Q

12. Stp on the bl of each foot, R and L, and on the count 'and 3', so that your feet are now in a parallel position and about shoulder width on the floor. Follow this with a hl-br with the R, a hop on the L and a stp, R over L, to land in the R. The counts for this are 'and 4 <u>and</u>'; this is syncopation because you are landing on an 'and' rather than a number.

Remember:

Syncopation is the use of these accents or stresses in an unusual way, so that an interesting rhythm emerges; we accent alternately on numbers as well as the other parts of the rhythm, the 'and' and the 'a'.

---

13. To finish this bar, do a shfl stp-hl stp on 'a6 and a 7' with the L and landing across with the R on '7'. (See the whole of figure 13.7.) Wait again on the '8, 1'.

I wonder if it is now possible to do this bar on the other side? Of course! You say, of course I can; I am now a tap dancer! (See figure 13.8.)

14. To repeat, then, do a to-hl on L and R, and on the counts 'a2'; stp onto the L and R bl of foot to be in a parallel position, 'and 3'; do a hl-br L, followed by a hp on the R, a stp on the L, 'and 4 and'. Finish with a shfl stp-hl stp on 'a6 and a 7' with the R; land across the R with the L on '7'.

15. Stp out to R side with the R on '8', *but* leave the L off the floor! (See figure 13.8 and picture 13.6.)

At this point do the Relax, Remind, Rewind, Repeat mantra in your head and go over it again with the tracks on the CD. We are half-way through this first dancing amalgamation. Let's continue, shall we?

16. Bring the L behind the R to land on the bl and stamp on the R, because you are now going to do the train step beginning with this stamp! In fact you are about to do *two* lots of them. So, using the counts '1 and 2 and 3 and 4 and 5 and 6 and 7 (and 8 and) 1 and 2 and 3 and 4 and 5 and 6 and 7 and 8 and 1' (phew!) – yes, that's right, it is repeating without a break and is exactly the same and on the same foot, too. (See figures 13.9 and 13.10.)

> **Note two things here:**
>
> First, you are doing the train step with the front *flat* foot stamping on the 'and', so it will feel different. If you remember, this front flat step was taught on the number and the two steps in the back, on the 'and a'. At least, I always began with the front step on the number.
>
> Second, look at the numbers in brackets (and 8 and). These are the connecting steps and numbers to get you into the repeat. For these three counts just step in place (R L R) and you should find the steps naturally go into the repeat, if you do the same with your L behind on the '1' again. Don't forget, it is exactly the same foot placings the second time.

picture 13.6   Step out to R side

17. The way to get out of this sequence now is to do the last 'and 8 and' in place as before, but landing the '1', on the L, quite heavily in front and, in fact, with a full foot stamp! This forms your first step in the next bar, clever, eh? Clever, because this is the drop you require for the first step of the Shim Sham 4, on the L. It is, of course, going to be done on '1' and not, as taught, on '8'. Do it anyway, and add the break too, which will also fall on the '1'. (See figures 13.11 and 13.12.)

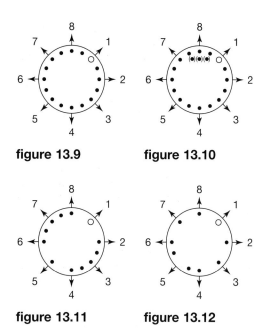

figure 13.9   figure 13.10

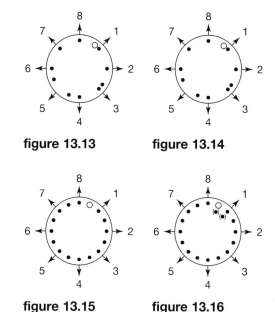

figure 13.13   figure 13.14

figure 13.11   figure 13.12

figure 13.15   figure 13.16

18. End this break in the L this time, and not with the L resting (on count 8).

Don't worry that a step like the Shim Sham now has a different number as its beginning. Any time step, such as this one, can begin on any number, but it has to be taught on the traditional number '8'.

If we do one more phrase of four bars, we will be achieving a natural rounded set of figures and counts that will fit most standard jazz pieces and certainly the one included on the CD. So, here we go for the finish of this first tap dance amalgamation.

19. Do a tp-stp R into the right-hand diagonal corner of the space you are dancing on and put down the R hl also for 'a1 2'; do another tp-stp but to the left-hand diagonal corner on 'a3'. The hl will again follow as before, but it has to be connected to the *next* sound which will be the bl of the R, landing behind the L. The effect here is to do a hl-bl, L-R, on '4 and'.

20. The R hl is off the floor, so you can repeat this hl-bl action, R-L, and bring the L behind the R to land, 'and 6'. To finish, stp to the side on the R and close L to it, '7 8'. (See figures 13.13 and 13.14.)

To finish, you are going to go through a series of paddles, 3s, 4s, 5s, 6s, 7s and 8s!

21. Beginning R then L, with 'and 1 and 2 and 3 and', do one 3bt pdl; follow this with one 4bt pdl. Now do one 5bt pdl, a 6bt pdl, a 7bt pdl, and an 8bt pdl. Use each foot in turn – R L R L R L – and finish with a stamp on '1', on the R. I will rely on your newfound knowledge of the rhythm clock to see that the rhythm is all of one kind and that if you do this all correctly, you will end on '1'. The 'and 1' in brackets serves as our ending. (See figures 13.15 and 13.16.)

That concludes Amalgamation 1. Don't forget, practice makes it perfect. Relax, Remind, Rewind, Repeat … Repeat … Repeat … Repeat …!

Amalgamation 2

This amalgamation has a good Latin feel about it and this musical style can actually help with tap because of its even musical character. We just simply divide the tempo in half and keep the counting to a minimum; just saying 'and 1 and 2 and 3 and 4…'. That is not to say we cannot syncopate, because we actually will find it easier on this even base. Let's try the next routine to this Latin groove. If you enjoy this kind of music do please try to imbue into the dance some of this unique feeling; you will find the steps flow more easily.

1. On the R, do a 4bt pdl and start the count on '1'; do it also on the L. Now do an 8bt pdl, which will again be on the R. This will end in the R heel on '8 and', so freeing the L to repeat all again, on the other side. (See figures 13.17 and 13.18.) On our rhythm clock, as you can see, the numbers and spaces are filled in right around.

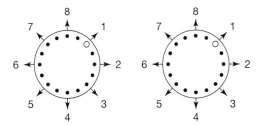

figure 13.17   **figure 13.18**

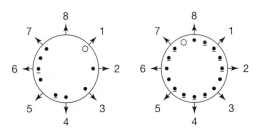

figure 13.19   **figure 13.20**

2. Following on from this easy start, now do some 3bt pdls beginning R, but this time using some syncopation, like so: '1 2 3 4 <u>and</u> and 6 and 7'. These will feel quite unusual to do, as though you are going at different speeds on each foot. This is because part of it is using cross-phrasing, using three sounds but in an even (two-sound) rhythm. Emphasize the <u>underlined</u>.

3. It's actually the same thing done three times with the first 3bt pdl done evenly, the second is the most unusual, done on '4 and and', and the third done quickly at twice the speed of the first. Hope that helps! Do R then L then R. (See figure 13.19.)

4. Now do shfl bl-ch bl-ch, shfl bl-ch bl-ch, shfl bl-ch, beginning with the shfl on the L foot and going to the R side. Count it so: 'and 8 <u>and 1</u> <u>and 2</u> and 3 <u>and 4</u> <u>and 5</u> and 6 <u>and 7</u>.' You will see it is in an even count and should be done in this way *and* with the Latin hips and feeling you can bring to it. Again emphasize the <u>underlined</u> to bring forward this particular syncopation; some good examples of the 'and' being stressed. (See figure 13.20.)

5. Now for the even time step that the double time step provides. Do this on the L side, beginning with the L, and do the break too. Count it, however, beginning on the 'and 8' and not the usual '8 and'. Carry on until you finish the break with the bl-ch on the '6 and', R-L.

6. If you do two more bl-ch, R-L R-L, this will bring you to the drop on '1', which is the next bar. (See figures 13.21 and 13.22.)

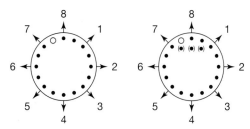

figure 13.21   **figure 13.22**

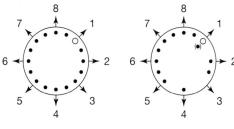

figure 13.23   **figure 13.24**

7. Next, do some five-beat paddles (you can do it … keep trying!). You will need three 5bt pdls here. But first, begin these with a drp on '1', on the R.

8. From this heavy downward stamp on the R, free the L to do the first 5bt pdl. Do this, and two more, using the count – you have probably guessed by now –'and 2 and 3 and 4 and 5 and 6 and 7 and 8 and', an even count. (See figure 13.23.)

9. On the next count of '1', which is on the R, do again a stamp but to the R side. Now, do a p-up stp, '2 <u>and</u>' on the L, to land behind the R. We have syncopated out the '3' so do two stamps on the R and the L, '4 5'. Your feet should now be in parallel, shoulder-width apart and the weight is in the L.

10. Now do a p-up stp on the R and again on the L, backwards but again with the weight ending in the L. You are now on the balls of both feet and ready to do a shfl hp-stp on the R. The counts for all of this are 'and 6 and 7 and 8 and 1' (which is the first count of the next bar). (See figure 13.24.) We are now half-way through this amalgamation.

11. On '1', which is your stp on the R, (land this in front) put your weight into it to free the L to do a shfl-stp '2 and 3', crossing behind the R; follow this with a stp on the R, to the R side on '4'. Follow this with a stp on the L slightly to the L side '5'; shfl stp R to land behind the L '6 and 7'; stp L on '8'. (See figure 13.25.)

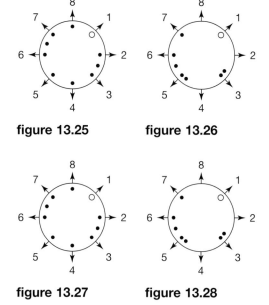

figure 13.25   **figure 13.26**

figure 13.27   **figure 13.28**

The next is easy because it is back to our basic single steps, but with rhythm.

12. Step R on the '1', and do the following rhythm.

'1 __ a3 __ a5 and 6 7 __, with stp, bl-ch, bl-ch bl-ch clap. (See figure 13.26.)

13. Now repeat figures 13.25 and 13.26 again but to the other side, i.e. beginning with the stp on '1' with the L this time. Do it exactly the same but on the other side. (See figures 13.27 and 13.28.)

14. For the last four bars, do the Shim Sham 1 on R from the beginning, to the end of the **break**. Go on the '8', as taught, starting with shfl-stp, shfl-stp, shfl bl-ch, shfl-stp and carry on to the end. The first bar is '8 and 1 2 and 3 4 and 5 and 6 and 7'. Go back if necessary to the Chapter 11 featuring Shim Sham 1. (See figures 13.29–13.32.)

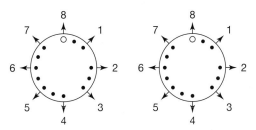

figure 13.29   **figure 13.30**

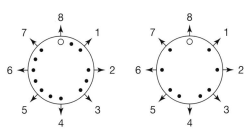

figure 13.31   **figure 13.32**

That's the end of this one and I hope you are still with me to do the last one! Try to organize your brain to do **Trap, Clap, Tap** as often as you can.

We have now reached the last routine in this book and I have chosen a typically sounding show tune (track 57 of the CD). The difference between the first two, one of a jazz nature and one of a Latin nature, is not too broad. A show tune is just what it says – it has to look 'showy' and not just rely on rhythm alone. It is difficult enough to teach sound in a book and I think I have accomplished that aspect. To teach style as well, however, that's a different set of marks I think you'll agree! We can but try!

With a show routine the arms and body may have to come to the fore and I hope you will use the photographs from now on to see yourself in that routine, in that show, on that stage. Don't worry, you won't need a costume! Unless you feel like wearing one, of course!

Another main feature is the use of dynamics in the musical arrangement. Often the overture to a show acts as a taster of what is to come. It will use snippets of the show's songs and act as an introduction. The idea is to enthuse the listener of course. Also, this overture-type of music can use different shades within its short period, going from one to another without pause.

A particularly good feature to make use of is something called 'tacit' and a smaller, shorter version of it, called 'stop time'. My understanding of tacit is it is a silence over a bar or more of music. Stop time is a more natural and spontaneous pause with a jazz feel and musicians use this feature almost constantly. It is part of syncopation itself, to use these pauses of one, two or three counts here and there throughout, while playing a piece.

It is also a perfect gift for the tap dancer! There is absolute joy to be found in a piece of music that actually makes a space for you to fill with your very own rhythmical contribution.

Having all of this in mind, and with the reminder that dance pieces require much more description, I hope you feel, when you do the last routine in this book to the last tune on the CD, that you have made your way down this very skilled path to enlightenment(!).

Amalgamation 3

1. See picture 13.7 for the very first position of this routine. You will notice it is a step with no sound but with a *position* of the R knee highly lifted and crossing. Also see the arms, hands and fingers in a stretch downwards and forward and with a finger snap. This opening position is on '1'.

picture 13.8   Count on '5'

picture 13.7   Count is on '1', a lifted position

2. Continue, and put the foot down for '2' across the L foot. Graduating forward slightly, stp on the bl of the L and R foot on '3 4'. Repeat this on the other side but change the arm to one stretched above your head (picture 13.8) and count it straight as you go '1 2 3 4 5 6 7 8' for each side. Because you lift the knee and do the arm position on the '1; 5; 1; 5' and therefore achieve no sound, this will give us that missed beat that adds to the flavour of an interesting and building rhythmic combination.

3. Don't forget to come forward here and repeat each side exactly. Do four of these figures (see figure 13.33 and 13.34) but on the fourth one, stop on the count of '7', on the R foot. Bring the arm down to your side on '6 7'. You are now standing feet parallel with arms momentarily down to your sides and your weight in the R. Wait on the count of '8'.

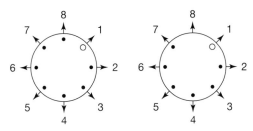

figure 13.33	figure 13.34

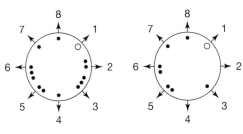

figure 13.35	figure 13.36

4. Now, but only if you feel confident, try to do a Maxie Ford. You must do a heavy spr down onto the L on '1' and shfl the R to the side as described in Chapter 12 Other famous steps. Do the step and the counts as described but finish with the feet apart. This will bring you to the end of figure 13.35.

5. With your feet apart, do a hl bt on the R, another hl bt on the R, followed by two bl-ch L-R, L-R, plus another hl bt on the R. The counts for this are: '1 __3 __ a5 a6 7'.

6. On the end of this do a *shunt* (which I have not described so far, but which follows below) on '8'. (See figure 13.36.)

7. The shunt is an effective movement and sort of breaks the rule of not being able to use a foot if you are already in it with your full weight. You are in this foot and you are flat, so *push* the foot slightly along the floor with a small movement. It is not a hop or a stamp or a step – it's a shunt! And I grant you, a funny word to describe it, right?

8. Your L foot will be off the floor and your weight fully into the R, rather like the position in picture 13.6.

9. Now go on to look at pictures 13.9a–c. The body is really quite forward and down, the arms are swinging naturally and the R leg is out to the side and scything backwards round and behind the L in a progressive rear-going action. Study the movement before going onto the steps themselves, which are not difficult.

10. Spr down into the L and shoot the R out to the side and into this round action to the back. Do this on '1' (picture 13.9a). During this and at about half way round, do a hl on the L on '2' (picture 13.9b). The R should continue round and land on '3' (see picture 13.9c). This stp on '3' is the first step of the repeat on the other side. Use a low scything action going to the back and on the counts '1 2 3 4 5 6', which is three times. Note that the heels are on the counts '2 4 and 6'. (See figure 13.37.)

picture 13.9a   R about to go round to the back

11. Carry on bringing the R round behind the L to step 'behind, side, forward' ... R L R ... and on '7 8 1'. If you know any ballet, you will recognize this as a 'pas de bourrée'. You should be in a crossed over – R over L – position and are on the count of '1'.

picture 13.9c   R now round to back

picture 13.9b   R continuing to go round

12. This count of '1' should be a heavier stp and in fact should be a spr down into the floor *and on the ball* to facilitate the next thing you are to do. Look at picture 13.10 and you will realize that you are to hp off the floor on the R after doing a brush with the L hl out to the L side and with L across, then R out into parallel after hopping.

13. Do this action to the counts '1 <u>and</u> __ a 3 4', repeating '5 <u>and</u> __ a 7 8'. The underlined is the hl-br and is a strong accented sound. Use the counts shown in figure 13.38.

Now for some tacit and stop time!

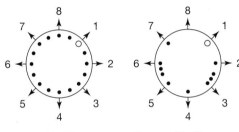

figure 13.37   **figure 13.38**

figure 13.39   **figure 13.40**

picture 13.10   Brush hop

14. I hope you have practised your Scissors and One, because it's about to come up, and on the R foot. Spr down onto a flat R foot, then execute the Scissors and One step to the counts of: '1 and 2 and 3 and 4 and 5 and 6 and 7 and 8 (and 1)'. The last two steps (L and R), mean you have landed again on the R foot. However, this time really get that foot flat on the floor with a great and full sound. (See figure 13.39.)

15. Now to finish the phrase with a flourish! Bring the L into the R and do a 4bt crmp rl, leading with the L. Remember the cramp rolls are using four beats *cramped* together so the count comes out as: '2 and a 3'.

16. Do this 4bt crmp rl and a stamp on the L immediately after it, on count '4'. Repeat, but on the other side and don't forget the '4' is the same flat as the '1' above, and so you only have to do the 4bt crmp rl. This cramp roll will, of course, be on '5 and a 6'. By now doing a stamp again, on the R, you will finish the phrase on the count of '7'. (See figure 13.40.)

Obviously, the music will have virtually stopped here, because of the tacit, and you will only hear a kind of supporting beat in the background, just to keep you in time. The steps are thus highlighted and you are on your own! But you can safely and honestly say that you are now a part of the whole picture – you are a rhythmic arrangement over the top of other rhythmic arrangements and you are involved and completing the picture. Well done if you have got this far. Amazing if you have come from a beginner! But we are just half-way with this one!

A good trick, but one that could make you feel somewhat ill, is to now do the whole thing on the other side! Well, at least you will have a double-length routine but using steps that, in a sense, you already know, if you see what I mean. You can think about this and then set about trying to do it. What will probably happen is you will start to do it and find quite quickly that it feels uncomfortable on the other side. It is precisely this feeling that you must conquer, because if you can do this you are truly building yourself a tap dancer's brain. A brain that has to think quickly and clearly without hesitation. No wonder some professional dancers say those words that began this book, that if you can't tap dance, you can't dance. Let's say it the other way round – if you *can* tap dance, you can dance any other dance!

Let me assume you have either done the other side, in which case congratulations, because you have your 16 bars! Or, you have not, and you have merely done the first side as just described. I want to continue this last piece to get you to 16 bars for the routine. But I digress … let us see what more we can do, eh?

17. Do a to on the L, behind and crossed over the R on '8'. Try to get a real feeling of twisting here, using your body and arms as in picture 13.11. Now a hl R on '1', stp L and R and L on the balls in the weaving pattern (described in an earlier combination) on '2 3 4'. You must work the weaving to the L side and your feet will go forward, back, side as you travel to the L side. Now kick the R hl over the L and hp on the L before landing on the R and on the ball. These counts must be taken from the '4', which is a step on the L, because the step and the heel kick are on the '4 and'. It is easier to do the two things together. The hp is on the next 'and', the following and last step is on '6'. Wait on '7'. (See figure 13.41.)

picture 13.11 L toe behind, crossed over

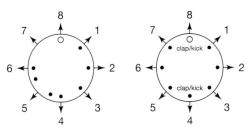

figure 13.41   **figure 13.42**

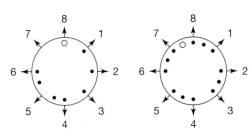

figure 13.43   **figure 13.44**

18. Clap on the count of '8' and kick also on this count with the L and out to the L side (see picture 13.12a). Step L R L and do these behind, side and then forward crossed over R and travelling to R. The counts are '1 2 3'. Repeat this on the other side, beginning with a clap on '4' (picture 13.12b) and go on to the counts '5 6 7', but do the steps R L R more back, together and forward and not travelling. You should now be in the R again and on a flat foot. (See figure 13.42.)

19. Figure 13.43 will make it easy now to replicate figure 13.41. Do the same thing, to L, hl R, stp L and R and again stp L and kick the hl R over the L, just as you did before. Hp L and land on the R on '6'. Don't forget to do the body twist at the beginning as the picture suggests (picture 13.11). Wait on '7'.

picture 13.12a   Clap/kick

picture 13.12b   Clap/kick

20. Do a stamp on the L and stamp R to have feet shoulder-width apart. This is now the first step of the Shim Sham 3 – a double stamp on 'and 8' – but of course the first p-up will be on the L side and you only need to do the first part. Refer to Chapter 11 The Shim Sham Shimmy and when you are ready, and have done the Relax, Remind, Rewind and Repeat mantra, have a go at adding this one measure of 8 counts to the routine. (See figure 13.44.)

Well, we are now at the point of the big finish again! Before we complete, let me say that I realize you are probably not dancing this on a stage! Or even a dance studio floor; most likely you are trying to dance this where you are living. I hope you have a mirror because this routine is our 'show routine'.

Nevertheless, I think it has been good to do a more complex and bigger piece. We can finish with a couple of easy but travelling steps.

21. Do a triple time step on the R. Your last R foot was a stp on '7'. You will, therefore, have to do a quick weight change stepping onto the L on 'and' to free the R, to do shfl (8 and) to begin the time step. Refer to the rhythm clock for the timing, but you should already know this of course! (See figure 13.45.)

22. Do not do the break. Instead, do a very special and famous step (I mean, among us Hoofers now!) called The Shorty George! That's right, you heard it correctly. It is an old Lindy Hop term, invented around the time that the Lindy was being danced (about 1926 to 1945). It is a really nifty walking step that uses the knees as – hopefully – you can see in pictures 13.13a and b.

picture 13.13a   The 'Shorty George'

picture 13.13b   The 'Shorty George'

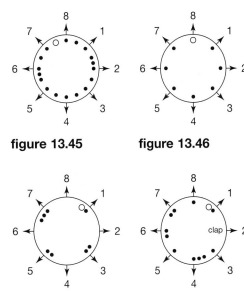

figure 13.45   **figure 13.46**

figure 13.47   **figure 13.48**

23. Do this step for 8 counts, a straight 8 1 2 3 4 5 6 7 . (See figure 13.46.) It begins R.

24. Now do a jump from side to side. Go to the R first, doing a spr onto the R, closing L to it; a spr onto the L, closing R to it. Repeat those two things for the rhythm in the clock. (See figure 13.47.)

25. The last thing to do is stamp stamp 'a 1', R L; clap on '2'; do a dbl pl-bk on '3and a 4'; drp onto R and finish with shfl bl-ch L, stamp L on '5 a6 a7 8'. (See figure 13.48.)

Just to remind you, don't expect too much at the beginning. You will need to practise and be prepared to get it wrong for a while. I still do that, you know – there is no escape from the work that eventually pays off!

Major point:

Doing a tap routine is quite a feat, I assure you. It is one thing to learn individual steps and to put them sort of side by side; it is quite another to join them *in a dance way*, with all the attendant moves with style and arms and directions.

14 make up your own

In this chapter you will learn:

- how to put dance steps together by yourself
- that music is the key
- rules to remember from now on.

Let me take you right back to one of the early chapters and home in on *why* you are tap dancing. Why do you want to play *any* instrument? What is it about us that produces rhythm anyway?

Well, it's the same thing that drives us to improve ourselves at any skill. I referred to tap dance as a skill and I am sure you are now convinced it is, if you have read the whole of this book and have managed to perform some or all of the steps. It takes patience and courage and determination and time to learn anything to do with music and one could sympathize with those who regard music a fiendish invention! Especially the five-year-old given a violin to learn!

But you – you are different. You are expressing something inside that has always been there and you have the ability to bring out. By just doing this thing called tap you are listening to yourself, getting in touch, feeling the beat. Bearing this in mind, and having learnt much of this book and the steps in it, you may now want to 'play your own tunes'. You may now want to play the instrument in your own way. Is that not *why* you are learning to tap dance?

It just is not like any other form of dance. It has sound and vision; it has a kind of soul that needs to express through rhythm. And it is personal! It is like writing, like painting, like designing your home interior or like making your own rugs! It becomes personal. Even when doing it with the rest of a class, it is still personal. It is ours and that is why we love to do it.

So if you love to play your instrument, why not write your own tunes? Why not paint what you want to paint, now that you have learnt to paint in class? Why not produce your own pieces with the skill now at your toe-tips? Why not indeed?

I will now give you some guidance on how to put dance steps together – choreography. What you can achieve is only as limited as you want it to be. One thing I can guarantee, though, is that you must be able to listen to a great degree … to music, yourself, your mind, your rhythm trying to get out.

The music is the key

If you can listen to music and hear, really hear the musical phrasing, the dynamics, the arrangements and the beat, you have a chance. It is good to do this because even though you have the steps I have taught you, it will all come out differently because it will be in your style, and not anyone else's.

Listen to the music that moves *you*. It must have a beat that moves your feet! You'll know if this happens and you will then not stop practising. It will be your routine to your music and that is the greatest.

Listen to the beat; fiddle around a bit; do your favourite step again and again. Remind yourself of a particular step you picked up quite quickly in the book. It could be that you became quickly adept at paddles. They are great for showing off, with such little effort. You can go fast with them and cross rhythm patterns easily and constantly. Just copying the melody of one of your songs or pieces at home with this step is a good start.

The 'tune' is crucial to learning because it is doing the job of organizing the rhythm for you. All you have to do is copy it. Later on you can put your own rhythm on the top of this tune. This will depend on your own feelings about the music, yourself and your interpretation.

Remember:

I believe we all have rhythm and I know you have. Do not think otherwise. It simply does not matter that it's not perfect for some time. I am always amazed at beginners or other lower level class members who sometimes say to me, 'But I don't sound as good as you', after my just congratulating them on doing something right! Really, I ask! And me only doing this for 30 years, too! Against your 30 minutes, what can I say? Go up to your karate instructor and say something similar ... if you dare!

I always say that in a class people are there to pick up steps to take home to practise. To not get them right then and there is actually all right. When I was with my teacher I simply could not wait to get home to practise. That is where the work is actually done. And guess what? You are already at home! If you are reading this at home I mean. Well, you get my drift, right?

A few rules then:

- Really listen *in* to the music you are practising to.
- Find the *tempo*, the *melody* and the *bar* endings.
- *Count* it all for a while, just using 1 to 8 (use a 4/4 mainly).
- *Tap* your feet along with the *tempo*.
- *Tap* your feet along with the *tune*.
- Try a couple of steps you find easy to do, to the music.
- Think of 'addition' of steps and don't try to be clever at first.
- Get to four bars and repeat.
- **Trap, Clap, Tap.**
- **Relax, Remind, Rewind, Repeat,** everywhere, anywhere.

conclusion

Throughout all of this I have tried to imagine the sort of person you are! As everyone – from Uncle Sam to Aunty Lily and all their little Toms, Anns and Dereks – seems to come into a tap class, I imagine you as all of them! Because everyone can tap dance – er, hold on a minute, that's perhaps a little too optimistic. I mean everyone comes in, but it isn't quite true that everyone comes back! So what do I do to get them to come back? Good question.

It is certainly the case that if you don't give it a try, you will never find out. One of the problems I always find is with the *perception* of this dance and the *reality*. From outside the studio door it looks really quite easy! That's because once anything is learnt, it becomes easier, and it is reasonable to say that people who have been to a class on just two occasions, are not technically beginners any more – quite straightforward so far then.

But we can be quite resistant to learning anything nowadays, it seems, and we all have experienced the 'want to do it *now*' feeling. You may not believe this but there are people who do expect instant results. In dance, instant results are not an option, I'm afraid! The perception and the reality are just not the same and I see on the faces of some, that they will not be coming back soon into my class. Pity, because I am a good teacher, and I can get you to tap dance. If you let me.

If you have managed to master a great deal of this book's steps and notes I must say a big congratulations. Just being able to do the Shim Sham from the beginning – or the Maxie Ford – is a great achievement! To learn them from a book is amazing; to learn them from *my* book is very flattering. And I hope you have. But, you know, the place to learn is in the tap studio.

For instance, give me – and yourself – a chance and turn up in shoes that will make a sound! Not trainers or ballet shoes or stilettos or socks! Would you turn up to a guitar lesson without your guitar? No!

This book is a good start to letting me teach you to tap dance. I have thrown in lots of different ways to learn and sometimes turned things around a little to deliberately exercise the corpuscles in your muscles! You have to meet me half-way though, and I know you know this really. I have confidence in you; now you must have it in yourself as you Teach Yourself to Tap Dance *further*.

The last word then, is: *Listen*. To the beat in everything; to the rhythm in everything; to the music in your soul and in your head, to yourself when you are finally tap dancing! Let Yourself Go ...!

Derek Hartley, 2007

Go to a class! Or do as I did, private lessons. Check out the internet because I am amazed at the number of people giving tap lessons. They will not always be good and some are particularly moribund in their approach and style. Use the advice in Chapter 01 'Where', to check out what the teacher is teaching. You could be lucky … you could come across someone I have taught in the past! Or someone that my wonderful friend Diane Hampstead has taught (once you have been taught by Diane, you remain taught!). After all, it's what I have been saying all along in this book … learn from the person if you can, and not the page.

This is not a contradiction here. I do realize you are reading this! But *I am from* the 'learning from the person' school and therefore I know what I am asking you to do. This is a book with several intentions in my opinion. It is written for those of you who are going to re-visit the tap dancing you once knew; to those of you who are just beginning; to those of you who are just reading because you like the subject and its attendant features such as jazz and that era; to those of you who want to exercise in a more cerebral mode. And to those of you who have found the rhythm in their soul and want to let it out. You are welcome to tap dancing!

You will know, as I did, when you walk into the room of a good teacher. You will hear the difference and the enthusiasm. I knew. You will see the intense concentration on the faces. My good friend Sue C. said the same about me and my class – and that was over 22 years ago! There you are, a perfect indication of how long you can expect to be doing this.

As for those people who look at the young and see they are absorbing steps at a very fast rate but who are themselves struggling to stay with the lesson at first, I say this is irrelevant. What is the hurry? For an adult, tap is perfect fare to digest. In fact, because of the sophistication in the history, the music and the timing and in the eloquence of the result, I believe it to be one of *the* forms of rescue from life's stressful game.

I just know you will agree if you take it slowly and deliberately.

Use this book as a sort of pre-emptive move towards going to your first class; you will know more of what to expect when you step into that studio and hear the teacher. I want you to be able to say, 'I know that step, because Derek Hartley taught it to me in his book!' It will all become familiar after such a short time, you will be quite surprised. If you can learn things from this book, you can certainly learn from the person, if they are good at their job.

Finally, then, and as promised, I must give you some help with what to do next, to actually take it further.

There are tap books on the market and I know they all say things in their own way, as we all do. Some books are good for just learning terminology and some are so good they are unreadable and show off to such an extent that only the writer can make out what is going on! Some books are good from an historical point of view and at least they are an enjoyable read. I have in no way tried to bamboozle you and I admit I have gone a little easy on you at times! I have also given you several ways to understand the counts and steps.

If you want to read further then go onto some good web pages and find some interesting titles. Why not also visit my website? I am on **www.dhp1.co.uk**.

Here are my suggestions of reading material:

Jazz Dance. The Story of American Vernacular Dance M.& J. Stearns. 1968. Macmillan, USA.
Tap! The Greatest Tap Dance Stars and their Stories R. E. Frank. 1990. Da Capo, USA.
The Souls of Your Feet, A. Gray. 1998. Grand Weavers Publisher, USA.
Inside Tap, A. Feldman. 1996. Princeton Book Co/Dance Horizon, USA.
Steps In Time, Fred Astaire. 1960. Heinemann, UK.
Tapping the Source. Tap Dance Stories, Theories and Practice, B. Bufalino. 2004. Cod Hill, USA.
The Book of Tap, Ames/Seigelman. 1977. McKay, USA.
Savion! My Life in Tap, S. Glover. 2000. Morrow & Co Inc, USA.

I have quoted from some of these titles. Others are for you to pursue in your quest to become a tap dancer.

list of titles

Teach yourself

From Advanced Sudoku to Zulu, you'll find everything you need in the teach yourself range, in books, on CD and on DVD.

Visit www.teachyourself.co.uk for more details.

Advanced Sudoku and Kakuro
Afrikaans
Alexander Technique
Algebra
Ancient Greek
Applied Psychology
Arabic
Aromatherapy
Art History
Astrology
Astronomy
AutoCAD 2004
AutoCAD 2007
Ayurveda
Baby Massage and Yoga
Baby Signing
Baby Sleep
Bach Flower Remedies
Backgammon
Ballroom Dancing
Basic Accounting
Basic Computer Skills
Basic Mathematics
Beauty

Beekeeping
Beginner's Arabic Script
Beginner's Chinese Script
Beginner's Dutch
Beginner's French
Beginner's German
Beginner's Greek
Beginner's Greek Script
Beginner's Hindi
Beginner's Italian
Beginner's Japanese
Beginner's Japanese Script
Beginner's Latin
Beginner's Mandarin Chinese
Beginner's Portuguese
Beginner's Russian
Beginner's Russian Script
Beginner's Spanish
Beginner's Turkish
Beginner's Urdu Script
Bengali
Better Bridge
Better Chess
Better Driving

Better Handwriting
Biblical Hebrew
Biology
Birdwatching
Blogging
Body Language
Book Keeping
Brazilian Portuguese
Bridge
British Empire, The
British Monarchy from Henry VIII, The
Buddhism
Bulgarian
Business Chinese
Business French
Business Japanese
Business Plans
Business Spanish
Business Studies
Buying a Home in France
Buying a Home in Italy
Buying a Home in Portugal
Buying a Home in Spain
C++
Calculus
Calligraphy
Cantonese
Car Buying and Maintenance
Card Games
Catalan
Chess
Chi Kung
Chinese Medicine
Christianity
Classical Music
Coaching
Cold War, The
Collecting
Computing for the Over 50s
Consulting
Copywriting
Correct English
Counselling
Creative Writing
Cricket
Croatian
Crystal Healing
CVs
Czech
Danish

Decluttering
Desktop Publishing
Detox
Digital Home Movie Making
Digital Photography
Dog Training
Drawing
Dream Interpretation
Dutch
Dutch Conversation
Dutch Dictionary
Dutch Grammar
Eastern Philosophy
Electronics
English as a Foreign Language
English for International Business
English Grammar
English Grammar as a Foreign Language
English Vocabulary
Entrepreneurship
Estonian
Ethics
Excel 2003
Feng Shui
Film Making
Film Studies
Finance for Non-Financial Managers
Finnish
First World War, The
Fitness
Flash 8
Flash MX
Flexible Working
Flirting
Flower Arranging
Franchising
French
French Conversation
French Dictionary
French Grammar
French Phrasebook
French Starter Kit
French Verbs
French Vocabulary
Freud
Gaelic
Gardening
Genetics
Geology
German

German Conversation
German Grammar
German Phrasebook
German Verbs
German Vocabulary
Globalization
Go
Golf
Good Study Skills
Great Sex
Greek
Greek Conversation
Greek Phrasebook
Growing Your Business
Guitar
Gulf Arabic
Hand Reflexology
Hausa
Herbal Medicine
Hieroglyphics
Hindi
Hindi Conversation
Hinduism
History of Ireland, The
Home PC Maintenance and Networking
How to DJ
How to Run a Marathon
How to Win at Casino Games
How to Win at Horse Racing
How to Win at Online Gambling
How to Win at Poker
How to Write a Blockbuster
Human Anatomy & Physiology
Hungarian
Icelandic
Improve Your French
Improve Your German
Improve Your Italian
Improve Your Spanish
Improving Your Employability
Indian Head Massage
Indonesian
Instant French
Instant German
Instant Greek
Instant Italian
Instant Japanese
Instant Portuguese
Instant Russian
Instant Spanish

Internet, The
Irish
Irish Conversation
Irish Grammar
Islam
Italian
Italian Conversation
Italian Grammar
Italian Phrasebook
Italian Starter Kit
Italian Verbs
Italian Vocabulary
Japanese
Japanese Conversation
Java
JavaScript
Jazz
Jewellery Making
Judaism
Jung
Kama Sutra, The
Keeping Aquarium Fish
Keeping Pigs
Keeping Poultry
Keeping a Rabbit
Knitting
Korean
Latin
Latin American Spanish
Latin Dictionary
Latin Grammar
Latvian
Letter Writing Skills
Life at 50: For Men
Life at 50: For Women
Life Coaching
Linguistics
LINUX
Lithuanian
Magic
Mahjong
Malay
Managing Stress
Managing Your Own Career
Mandarin Chinese
Mandarin Chinese Conversation
Marketing
Marx
Massage
Mathematics

ballroom dancing
craig revel horwood

- Do you want to learn to dance?
- Would you like enjoyable, easy-to-follow instructions?
- Are you looking for professional advice and tips?

From the tradition ballroom dances such as the Foxtrot, Waltz and Tango to Latin American dances like the Rumba, Samba and Jive, **Ballroom Dancing** covers it all. Each dance is explained using step-by-step instructions, photographs and diagrams that will ensure you are able to learn the basics quickly whilst having fun! Craig Revel Horwood, from the BBC's *Strictly Come Dancing*, makes this book lively and entertaining, with each step easy to learn – you will even get fit too! The accompanying audio CD contains all the tracks you need to learn and practise the steps to, as well as invaluable tips and advice from Craig himself.

Craig Revel Horwood is a highly acclaimed dancer and choreographer and features as a resident judge on the BBC's *Strictly Come Dancing* and *Celebrity Fame Academy*. He has danced in top stage shows, including *West Side Story*, *Cats*, *Miss Saigon* and *Crazy for You*. Craig has also directed and choreographed world-renowned shows including *Hey Mr Producer!*, *Spend, Spend, Spend*, *My One and Only*, *Calamity Jane* and *The Beautiful and Damned*. Most recently he has directed and choreographed the prestigious *Lido de Paris* and *The Lion King* for Disneyland Paris.

teach yourself

jazz
rodney dale

- Do you want to discover the musical and cultural history of jazz?
- Do you want to understand its musical structure and the way in which it is played?
- Are you looking to improve your understanding, appreciation and enjoyment of jazz?

Jazz is an essential guide for everyone whose imagination has been captured by the exciting world of jazz. Whether you want to know about the origins and development of jazz, or about important practitioners and bands, this book does it all. The audio CD helps to enhance your listening experience with examples of jazz styles and exercises to develop your understanding further.

Rodney Dale has been involved with jazz for over 40 years, including playing piano with a number of bands, organizing classes and workshops on jazz appreciation and writing books on the subject.

teach yourself

singing
rick guard

- Do you want to enhance your singing voice?
- Are you looking for proven advice from an enthusiastic instructor?
- Would you like to prove to yourself that you really can sing?

Whether you are an absolute beginner, a pop wannabe, a karaoke crooner, or want to add singing to your repertoire, **Singing** is for you. Friendly advice from your very own instructor will help you develop your voice and enable your talent to flourish. First learn the theory and technqiue on CD1, then use this with the vocal exercise programme included on CD2 to achieve the voice you've always dreamed of.

Singer/songwriter **Rick Guard** has performed extensively around the world, gaining top 20 hits in 11 countries. He has worked with some of the biggest names in show business and is about to release his album, *The Truth about Love*. He is also the creator of *Doctor Voice*.